Acknowledgements

I would like to thank everyone who has helped towards the preparation of this book, especially those who have given permission to use their ideas: Diana Allan, Jerome Boulter, Pat Collier, Cathy Gannon, John Higgins, Liz Lara, Anne Lawrie, Maria Meusz, Tim Murphey, Michael Rost, Sue Sheerin, and Verri Toste. Thanks too to John Green and Brian Quigley whom I have not been able to contact but would be pleased to hear from.

I would like to thank my students for trying out the ideas, and my colleagues for their help and advice. Special thanks to John Higgins for his help with computers.

I would also like to thank everyone at Oxford University Press for their inordinate patience and kindness in the long gestation period—you know who you are!

The author and publisher are grateful to the following for their kind permission to reproduce extracts and figures from copyright material:

An Post, the Irish General Post Office: advertisement from booklet on post office services.

Cambridge University Press: extract adapted from tapescript for M. Swan and C. Walter: *New Cambridge English Course* Book 3.

Dr Diana M. Henderson: extract from article written for *Edinburgh University Alumni Magazine* 1990.

Independent Television Association: job advertisement, 1992.

IPC Magazines Ltd: extract from *TV Times* 18–25 December 1995.

News International Newspapers Ltd: article 'Stop knocking the boss, Chris – he's behind you' from *The Sun* 19 December 1991.

NSPCC: photograph from advertisement, 1994.

Oxford University Press: extract from Tapescript 7 *Headway Intermediate* Student's Book, © Oxford University Press 1986.

The Reader's Digest Association Ltd: text of advertisement.

The Telegraph Group Ltd, Ewan MacNaughton Associates: chart from 'The Fish Forecast: Did he get it right?', *The Young Telegraph* June 1994, ©Young Telegraph 1994.

In memory of my father, Edmund White

Contents

The author and series editor

Over the last twenty years, **Goodith White** has worked in Italy, Finland, Singapore, Portugal and Ireland as a teacher and teacher trainer, with a brief diversion into publishing in the 1980s. From 1996 to 1999 she taught on the MSc TESOL course at the University of Stirling, and since 1999 has been lecturing on undergraduate and postgraduate courses in the School of Education, University of Leeds, mainly on B.A. programme for primary teachers in Oman.

Alan Maley worked for The British Council from 1962 to 1988, serving as English Language Officer in Yugoslavia, Ghana, Italy, France, and China, and as Regional Representative in South India (Madras). From 1988 to 1993 he was Director-General of the Bell Educational Trust, Cambridge. From 1993 to 1998 he was Senior Fellow in the Department of English Language and Literature of the National University of Singapore. He is currently a freelance consultant and Director of the Graduate Programme at Assumption University, Bangkok. Among his publications are *Literature*, in this series, *Beyond Words*, *Sounds Interesting*, *Sounds Intriguing*, *Words*, *Variations on a Theme*, and *Drama Techniques in Language Learning* (all with Alan Duff), *The Mind's Eye* (with Françoise Grellet and Alan Duff), *Learning to Listen* and *Poem into Poem* (with Sandra Moulding), *Short and Sweet*, and *The English Teacher's Voice*.

Foreword

The past decade has seen great changes in the importance accorded to the skill of listening in TESL/TEFL, and teachers now have available a wide range of published materials. The days of the 'great silence', when listening was very much the poor relation, are long past. However there is now a certain uniformity of approach to listening in many materials, which offer a relatively comfortable routine procedure (for the teacher at least) for dealing with the listening text.

This book arises from a feeling of unease and dissatisfaction with this situation, in which students are largely reduced to the role of passive 'overhearers', where most of the activity is initiated and controlled by the teacher and where listening is all too often dealt with in isolation from the other language skills.

It offers an array of fresh and original activities for helping students learn to listen. The emphasis is on giving the learners themselves a bigger role in the choice of materials and types of activity, and a greater control of the process. This implies an increased level of responsibility for their own listening development. It also helps to change their role as passive 'overhearers' to active participants in the process and makes the listening more personal to them. There is also a greater emphasis on reflecting on the process of listening as it unfolds in the activities, and on feeding the results of this reflection back into further work. The integration of listening with the other language skills is also given due attention.

This is not to say that the book turns its back on more familiar areas of listening work; the author includes activities to develop the familiar sub-skills or micro skills of listening. She has also included a section on project work, which encourages the learners to activate their listening in more sustained activities with an authentic pay-off.

The principal virtue of the book is its novel angle of approach to the map of listening, which makes the familiar landmarks appear in a new light. It will be a valuable resource to any teacher interested in reinvigorating their teaching of this key skill.

Alan Maley

Introduction

'Listening is not merely not talking … it means taking a vigorous human interest in what is being told us. You can listen like a blank wall or like a splendid auditorium where every sound comes back fuller and richer.'

Alice Duer Miller

The quotation above suggests that listening can be done in a narrow and limited way, or it can be done in a way that enriches communication. The activities in this book resulted from a growing feeling that I was selling my students short, both in the methods I was using to teach them the listening skill, and in the quality and scope of the listening ability they eventually acquired. Like most teachers I know, I tended to follow a number of familiar steps in a 'listening lesson', which had become comfortable and routine for me:

- do a 'warm up' on the topic of the listening passage
- set some 'gist' questions for the students to answer
- play the tape (it was usually an audio tape) once, and ask the students to answer gist questions
- check the answers
- set some tasks that require the students to listen for details
- play the tape again, probably once for each task
- check the answers
- use the topic or the language of the listening text as input for an 'extension' or 'transfer' activity in which the students use other skills, for example, writing, or speaking.

Over the years, I have begun to realize that there are a number of things wrong with this approach. Some of the features that trouble me are:

1 Not much time is spent actually listening to the tape

The students perhaps hear a two- to three-minute tape three or four times in the lesson at the most—a total of about 12 minutes' listening. The rest of the lesson is spent discussing the answers, and doing transfer activities.

2 Not much time is spent on analysing what went wrong

Teachers tend to focus on what the correct answers are to a listening passage, rather than why students fail to get them. We perhaps do not spend enough time looking at how students are mishearing or failing to hear, or whether there is in fact more than one possible answer. If enough students do not get the right answer, my typical reaction is to play that section of the tape once more, and hope that hearing it again will magically help the students to get the answer next time. I do not look at what might be causing the problem. This goes with a tendency for me as the teacher to focus on the product of listening (did the students get the right answers?) rather than the processes that are going on while they are actually listening.

3 The teacher takes on the sole responsibility for building up an understanding of the listening text in the students

The teacher pre-teaches vocabulary and sets tasks which he or she hopes will lead to comprehension and to the development of listening skills. This does not give the students much freedom to develop their own strategies for understanding; nor does it develop individual responsibility.

4 It assumes that there is only one way of listening to something

The task assumes that there are certain features of what is heard which are important, and these are the ones the questions focus on. However, we know that in real life, a number of people can listen to the same thing—for instance, a news broadcast—with different degrees of concentration, and remember different things from it, depending on their interests and reasons for listening. But we expect students in the classroom to all listen in the same way, and remember the same things.

5 Classroom listening very often puts students in the position of passive overhearers

This does not mirror real life, in which we can just as often be active participants in conversations, and can ask the speaker to adjust or repeat what he or she is saying if we do not understand. Too often in the classroom, students are listening to disembodied and unfamiliar voices on a tape recorder which they cannot stop, interrogate, or interact with in any way. The teacher is in control of the video or the tape recorder and he or she tends to stop it so that the students can do a task, rather than when they need to hear something again.

6 The tasks do not stress the links between listening and speaking

Listeners play a very important and active role in keeping conversations going, by showing interest and sympathy, and by causing speakers to modify or repeat things. The roles of speaker and hearer can change rapidly in a conversation, and listeners can become speakers at any moment, so learning how to listen in a second (or indeed a first) language is inextricably linked with learning how to speak. Good listeners make good speakers, and vice-versa. (Tony Lynch makes some good comments on the relationship between listening and speaking in his article 'The Listening–Speaking Connection'—see Bibliography.)

7 We often expect 100 per cent comprehension

A study by Bone (1988) of native speakers showed that people often listen at only 25 per cent of their potential and ignore, forget, distort, or misunderstand the other 75 per cent. Concentration rises above 25 per cent if they think that what they are hearing is important and/or they are interested in it, but it never reaches 100 per cent. Do we therefore expect too much of language learners, especially when there is no guarantee that the students are interested or motivated, since they have usually played no part in deciding what they listen to, or why they are listening? Readers who are interested in why we do not listen well may like to read Hargie *et al.* (1981)—see the Bibliography for details.

Other approaches

In an attempt to solve some of these problems, I have made some suggestions in this book for listening practice which the students control to a much larger extent than previously, and which can involve them in making their own recordings. The activities allow the students to do one or more of the following things:

- reflect on their problems in understanding and on strategies they could use to overcome those problems
- reflect on the links between listening and speaking
- become active participants in the listening process rather than passive overhearers
- control the equipment (tape recorder, etc.)
- give the instructions
- choose what they listen to
- design the listening tasks
- make their own listening materials.

The listening lesson becomes less predictable than the comforting set of steps I listed at the beginning of this introduction. It does take some getting used to. But I believe it pays off in terms of motivation, development of listening skills, and preparation for real-life listening.

Listening skills and strategies

There are an enormous number of sub-skills which go to make up the overall skill of listening, and each book seems to give different ones. Most experts distinguish between 'bottom–up' skills, which involve recognizing small bits of language, such as sounds and words, and 'top–down' skills, which involve using larger-scale clues, such as knowledge of the topic a speaker is talking about, the setting he or she is speaking in, or the gestures he or she makes, in order to make deductions about what is being said. Sometimes the 'bottom–up' skills are called 'micro' skills. Here is my own (subjective) checklist of sub-skills involved in listening, which shows the wide range of possible skills. Other teachers will have their own ways of categorizing the skills!

Perception skills

- recognizing individual sounds
- discriminating between sounds
- identifying reduced forms in fast speech (for example, elision and assimilation)
- identifying stressed syllables
- identifying stressed words in utterances
- recognizing intonation patterns.

Language skills

- identifying individual words and groups and building up possible meanings for them
- identifying discourse markers which organize what is being said, for example *then, as I was saying, as a matter of fact, to start with*.

Using knowledge of the world

- connecting groups of words to non-linguistic features such as expressions, gestures, or objects in order to get clues to meaning
- using knowledge of a topic to guess what the speaker might be saying about it
- using knowledge about the patterns that certain oral interactions typically take in order to predict what is being said, for example, ordering in a restaurant, making a telephone call.

Dealing with information

- understanding gist meaning (the overall idea of what you hear)
- understanding the main points
- understanding details, for example, train times
- inferring information which is not explicitly stated, or which has been missed.

Interacting with a speaker

- coping with variations among speakers, for example, differences in speed of talking and accent

- recognizing the speaker's intention
- identifying the speaker's mood/attitude
- recognizing the speaker's cues about things such as when to take a turn at speaking or when there is a change of topic
- predicting what the speaker will say next.

Good listeners need to be able to use a combination of sub-skills simultaneously when processing spoken language; the skills they will need at any particular moment will depend on the kind of text they are listening to, and their reasons for listening to it. Of course, language learners will not be very good at these skills to begin with, and teachers will need to teach them strategies for coping with what they have missed or misunderstood.

Strategies are efforts to compensate for uncertainties in understanding, and could include making inferences, realizing where misunderstandings have occurred, and asking for clarification. Students should need these strategies less and less as they get more familiar with the language and more competent at listening skills, although even very proficient native speakers will need to rely on them occasionally. Strategies can only really be taught effectively by interrupting the listening process and getting students to reflect on what they have just been doing, as they do for example in Activity 1.5, 'Up the garden path' or Activity 1.6, 'Interrupting'.

The approach I have taken in this book is to try to teach both strategies and sub-skills in conjunction with each other, and to grade the activities so that they move from 'easier' listening texts and tasks to more difficult ones. 'Easy' texts are shorter and feature familiar voices and topics. 'Easy' tasks are those which the students have designed or adapted and which allow them to be participants rather than in the more distant roles of audience or overhearers. The tasks and texts get more difficult in the later chapters because they are longer. They may feature unfamiliar voices and topics, and they place students in the more distant role of audience.

My students, who were kind enough to try out the activities with me, said that they used to be apprehensive in listening lessons, waiting for the tape recorder to be switched on and then concentrating very hard to try to do the tasks that had been set them. They felt that by giving them more input into, and control of, the listening they did, these kinds of activities removed anxiety and made listening a more enjoyable process. I noticed that a lot more of the class started participating, not just those who thought they knew the 'right' answer. I also gained more insight into what my students found difficult or easy in listening.

Last but not least, listening lessons became more fun for us, as I hope they will be for the classes who try out the activities in this book.

How to use this book

How the book is organized

The activities are arranged in such a way that they follow the guidelines above, and gradually:

1 Lead the students from listening to familiar voices and from shorter spoken messages which are designed for them as learners to longer ones which are designed for native listeners.

2 Show students how they can develop their own reasons and goals for listening, by designing their own listening texts and tasks.

3 Introduce students to all the skills which are involved in listening.

The activities are arranged like this:

1 Becoming a good listener

The activities in this chapter aim to make students aware of what a complex and active process listening is, and how it involves interacting with others as well as processing language. I have included activities which encourage students to think about how listening can help them in language learning, and ones which let them play a part in planning the listening they do inside and outside class.

2 Helping listeners to create their own listening texts and tasks

These activities encourage the students to design their own listening materials and tasks. They use familiar voices, such as themselves, their teachers, or other people that they know.

3 Micro skills

These activities give students help in decoding sound signals and coping with some of the features of fast speech. They focus on the 'small pieces' of a spoken message—sounds, stress, intonation, recognizing individual words, reduced forms, and so on, and on fairly short listening texts.

4 Adapting published materials

These activities encourage students to interact with published materials, and to become active participants in this kind of listening rather than just passive 'overhearers'. Many of the materials I use are dialogues and this chapter also focuses on the role of the listener in conversations and the relationship between listening and speaking.

5 Using authentic listening material

These activities give students practice in listening to the radio, television, lectures, and audio books—the kinds of things which native speakers listen to. They learn how to cope with the unpredictable and 'messy' things which happen in spoken English—false starts, utterances that change direction halfway, and so on, and also to react critically to what is being said. These activities help students to establish patterns for the extended kinds of listening texts they will be producing in Chapter 7.

6 Telephoning

The activities in this chapter lead students from making telephone calls to each other to 'real-life' calls where an unfamiliar voice is involved.

7 Listening projects

These are longer activities and projects which draw together all the sub-skills of listening and integrate listening with reading, speaking, and writing. They also put into practice, in a more extended form, the idea of students taking responsibility for learning, and for designing materials and tasks, which have been introduced in earlier chapters.

Pathways through the book

All levels of learner would benefit from doing some of the awareness-raising activities in Chapter 1 first, before they do any of the other activities. Lower-level students could do them through the medium of their own language. These activities show students that a wide range of skills is involved in listening, and that successful listening does not just mean understanding the main points of what is said—a view that has perhaps been over-stressed in the past. I would also advise teachers to sample some of the activities from Chapters 2 and 4 before they go on to the activities in Chapters 5, 6, and 7, which deal with real-life and extended listening. The activities in Chapters 2 and 4 aim to show students ways in which they can be active participants in the listening process, but they use simple, personal, short, and/or familiar listening passages to practise those methods. The activities in Chapter 3 can be done at any time, ideally interspersed with activities from other chapters. Being able to distinguish individual sounds, words, stressed syllables, and intonation patterns, and attach meaning to them, is an integral part of any kind of listening.

If you would like to improve the quality of the recordings that you and your students make, you may find it useful to read the advice on making recordings in Appendix 1 (page 133). One golden rule is always to do a short test to make sure your equipment is working before doing an activity which involves recording! Appendix 2 (page 135) contains some sources which I have found useful for developing my thinking in this fascinating area of teaching and learning. Finally, I wish you and your classes happy listening.

1 Becoming a good listener

The main aim of this chapter is to make the students aware of all the processes involved in listening. Language learners often think that all their difficulties in listening are due to their inadequate knowledge of the target language. But native speakers also experience problems with listening. Listening well involves motivation and concentration, and you can listen badly if you are not interested in the subject, or it is one that you do not know much about, or if there are a lot of distractions which make it difficult to focus on listening.

Listening is also closely connected with speaking. Being a good listener involves collaborating with speakers and taking an active role in asking for clarification when you do not understand. Some native speakers, particularly children and teenagers, are quite shy about doing this. Effective listening also involves empathizing with the speaker and trying to see things from his/her point of view. The listening activities in this chapter are designed to help the students to become aware of these social and psychological aspects of the listening skill which are often ignored when teaching the skill in a second language. They will also demonstrate time-saving strategies such as predicting what will be said next and inferring meaning.

The second aim of this chapter is to show the students how they can use listening to help them in their language learning in general. The activities towards the end of the chapter are designed to encourage the students to play an active part in choosing the materials and methods they can use to learn through listening, both inside and outside the classroom.

1.1 What's in a word?

LEVEL	**Intermediate and above**
TIME	**10 minutes**
AIMS	**To get the students to think about some of the different processes which can be covered by the word 'listening'.**

PROCEDURE

1 Write these sentences on the board (or give the students a photocopy):

---

1 She's just split up with her boyfriend, so I bet I'll have to listen to the whole story.

2 I keep telling him that his boss is not paying him enough, but he just won't listen.

3 I really like listening to Irish singers like Mary Black and Van Morrison.

4 Listen to me! I've had just about enough of your rudeness!

5 I usually listen to the news in the car on the way home from work.

6 Keep your mouth shut! Be on your guard! Enemy ears are listening to you! (public poster in World War I).

7 I find I always listen for my son coming back from the disco before I can go to sleep.

8 'Midland Bank—The Listening Bank' (advertisement).

Photocopiable © Oxford University Press

2 Ask the students to decide for each of the sentences:
   – *who* is listening (or, in the case of **2**, not listening!)
   – *why* they are listening
   – *what* they expect to hear.

3 Ask the students to rewrite the sentences without using the word 'listen'. They have to paraphrase using other words. (See the key below for some suggested answers.)

4 Discuss with the students what this activity has revealed about the number of different ways in which we can listen.

Key

Possible paraphrases for 'listen' could be:

1 sympathize with/follow/go over   2 believe
3 being entertained by   4 obey
5 pay attention to   6 checking on/monitoring
7 worry about, wait to hear   8 caring

Acknowledgements

This activity was inspired by and adapted from one in Michael Rost's *Introducing Listening* (1994: 1–2). Used with permission.

1.2 Tapefriends

LEVEL   **Elementary and above**

TIME   **30 minutes**

AIMS   **To show that listening is closely connected with speaking, and that what speakers say and the way they say it can make listening easy or difficult.**

MATERIALS   A tape recorder and if possible a microphone. The tape letter can also be videoed if you have access to a video camera.

PROCEDURE   1 Explain to the students that instead of writing a letter to a prospective penfriend, they are going to send an audio or video tape to introduce themselves. It is a good idea to make this a genuine activity if you can, and arrange to exchange the tape with another class of roughly the same level in another country, another school in the same town, or another class within the same institution. (See Appendix 2 for ideas on how to find penfriends.)

2 Tell the students that they are going to take it in turns to record themselves for one to two minutes. They are going to introduce themselves, say a little bit about their age, family, job, hobbies, and the town where they live. (This is an ideal revision activity for beginners just after they have learnt these basic language items.) The students should also say who they would like as a 'tapefriend'—boy or girl, age, interests, and so on. Give the students a few minutes to make notes on what they are going to say. They might also like to practise it with a partner.

3 The students take it in turns to record themselves. If the class is a large one, you may want to divide it up into groups, each with its own tape recorder, or spread the activity over a couple of classes.

4 Write the following questions on the board and then play the tape, while the class listen and note down their reactions:
   - *Who spoke fastest/slowest?*
   - *Who spoke loudest/softest?*
   - *Who said the most/the least?*
   - *Who had the clearest pronunciation?*
   - *Did anybody use any words you did not know? What were they? Could you guess the meaning?*
   - *Did you notice any mistakes? What were they? Did they make it difficult to understand what the speaker was saying?*
   - *Who was the most interesting?*
   - *Who would you like to have as a tapefriend? Does your answer to this question have anything to do with your answers to the other questions?*

5 Ask the class to share their responses to the questions in Step 4. This feedback needs to be conducted in a positive and sensitive way: it should not become too critical of individuals.

COMMENTS

1 Some classes enjoy this kind of peer observation and can do it in a co-operative and friendly manner. With other classes, you may prefer just to ask the students to compare their reactions in pairs.

2 The students will probably notice that the best and most interesting speakers are those who make the listener's job easier. This activity, for instance, often identifies people who are not using a very wide intonation range and who could sound rather monotonous and boring. It also identifies people who are speaking too slowly or too fast.

FOLLOW-UP

Before the students send the tape to another class, they might want to make an 'improved' version in the light of their discussion in Steps 4 and 5. They could also design a task for the other class to do with the tape, for example, a set of true/false or comprehension questions to answer after listening. If they are sending an audio tape, they could each send a photo of themselves, and ask the other class to guess which voices on the tape go with which photos.

1.3 Sounds of silence

LEVEL

All

TIME

5–10 minutes

AIMS

To focus totally on listening, and to improve concentration.

PREPARATION

With lower-level classes, before you do this activity, you might want to brainstorm some of the noises they think they might hear, since the students often find this area of vocabulary quite difficult. You may like to pre-teach or revise the use of the -*ing* form (gerund) to denote actions, for example 'eating', 'crumpling'.

PROCEDURE

1 Ask the students to close their eyes and concentrate totally for 30 seconds on listening to see how many sounds they can hear: footsteps in the corridor, a ticking clock, someone's stomach rumbling, and so on. You will tell them when the 30 seconds are up.

2 Ask the students which sounds they heard.

3 Ask the students to listen again with their eyes closed. This time you are going to perform an action, and they have to guess what you are doing from the sound they hear.

4 Do the action. Some suggestions are:
  - writing on the board
  - crumpling some paper and throwing it in the bin
  - opening the window
  - eating a sweet and crumpling the wrapper
  - jumping on the spot
  - drinking some water from a glass
  - pushing a chair under a desk
  - drumming your fingers on the desk.

COMMENTS

This is a good warmer to start a listening skills lesson.

1.4 Getting the frame

LEVEL

Lower-intermediate and above

TIME

10 minutes

AIMS

To use previous knowledge of a topic to understand a listening passage.

MATERIALS

Tape recorder; a recording of a listening passage

PREPARATION

Choose five survey questions on topics which are connected to the listening passage. They can be to do with facts or opinions: for example, for *New First Certificate Masterclass*, Unit 6, pages 84–5, you could use the following:
  - find out as much as you can on the topic of exams
  - find out people's attitudes to telling lies
  - find out what foods people hate eating
  - find out some information about famous footballers
  - find out if people have met someone famous, and what their reaction was.

PROCEDURE

1 Tell the students they are going to do a survey. Divide the class into five roughly equal groups, and give each group a survey question. The students circulate individually and find out as much as they can about their topic in 5 minutes. They can only ask members of other groups, not their own.

2 When the 5 minutes are up, the groups meet to pool the information they found out about their topic.

3 Each group elects a spokesperson, who tells the rest of the class what their group has found out.

4 Tell the class that they are going to listen to a recording which may mention some of the ideas and information which they have gathered. Ask the class to suggest three or four 'gist' (not

detailed) questions. They are going to listen to the tape and try to find the answers to these questions.

5 Play the tape. The students try to answer their questions.

6 Ask the students to say whether any of the information they found out proved useful in helping them to understand the tape. Point out (or elicit) that it is a good idea to use what you already know about a topic to help you to understand a listening passage.

1.5 Up the garden path

LEVEL   **All**

TIME   **10 minutes**

AIMS   **To encourage the students to predict what they will hear next.**

PROCEDURE

1 Tell the students that you are going to tell them a story, and that you will pause every now and then to ask them what they think is going to happen next. It might be a good idea to do a trial run first: read out the first sentence and elicit suggestions for what might come next.

2 Tell the story, pausing to let the students make their predictions. Here is an example I used with intermediate-level students. You will need to elicit/explain the meaning of the words 'monk' and 'monastery' before you tell this story. You could also ask the students what kind of story they expect when they hear these two words.

Brother John had been a monk for many, many years. He was very happy when his superior told him one day that he had a visitor.

Pause

He rushed to the lounge and found that his visitor was an old school friend, Andrew. They were talking happily about the good old days when suddenly, from somewhere in the monastery, there came a dreadful howling noise which made their blood run cold.

Pause

'What on earth was that?' asked Andrew. 'I am sorry, Andrew', said Brother John, 'but I have sworn to keep it a secret. Because you are not a monk, I cannot tell you'. After another half an hour, Andrew left, still wondering what the mystery was. He promised to visit his old friend again soon. But ten long years passed before they met again. In the meantime …

Pause

Andrew had become a monk too. The first thing he said when he met Brother John was …

Pause

'Now I am a monk you can tell me what is going on here. For ten long years I have been wondering what that dreadful howling meant'.

Pause

So Brother John told him.

Pause

I'm sorry I can't tell you, because you aren't monks.

FOLLOW-UP 1   For this story, the students suggest what the howling noise was.

FOLLOW-UP 2   In pairs, the students construct similar stories to tell each other. You could also play short excerpts of news stories, talks, or dialogues and ask the students to say what the topic is and to predict what will be said next. This is good practice for one of the possible listening tasks in the Cambridge First Certificate examination.

1.6 Interrupting

LEVEL   **Elementary and above**

TIME   **5–10 minutes**

AIMS   **To encourage the students to ask for clarification and to realize it is not always their fault when they do not understand; to guess the meaning of words they have missed.**

PREPARATION   Find or write a short text that the students will find interesting, and which is at their level. It should be 'written to be spoken', so make it fairly 'chatty'. When you read the text to the class, you are going to obscure some of the words by coughing or mumbling. Underline the words which you are going to obscure—it is not a good idea to have too many, or the students will find it quite difficult to follow. One for every 20 or so words of the story is enough. You will find out the best words to obscure by reading the story out loud to yourself. For intermediate students, I have used this:

The Ghost Ship

The story I'm going to tell you is a ghost story. Do any of you like or read ghost stories?… Well, this particular story is rather unusual because it is not about a house with <u>ghosts</u> in it, like most of the stories, it is about a ship with a ghost. And it happened fairly recently, in the 1970s, to be precise, so the people who were involved in the story are still <u>alive</u>. The story starts when the ship was built in Cork, in Ireland, and it was <u>bought</u> by a man called Jimmy O'Donnell, who used it for fishing. Everything was going <u>fine</u> until one day, it was a freezing cold day in December 1976, three of the <u>crew</u> were pulling in the fishing nets over the side of the ship, when one of them got caught in the net and was dragged overboard. Before anyone had a chance to save him, he <u>drowned</u> in the icy water. After this awful tragedy, Jimmy <u>O'Donnell</u> lost his taste for fishing, his heart just was not in it anymore, and he sold the <u>ship</u>.

The ship next turned up in the north of England, at a place called Bridlington. It had a new <u>captain</u>, called Mick Laws, who was really excited about his new <u>job</u>. But, as he was to say later, the next few months, instead of being good, were destined to be the worst of his life. Things kept going wrong with the boat, things that you couldn't explain. And the cabin on the boat was always icy cold, even though they tried everything they could to make it <u>warmer</u>—new heating, oil stoves, fires. Then the captain had a terrible <u>experience</u>. He was lying on his bed, going to sleep one <u>night</u>, when he saw the side of his mattress being pulled down, as if somebody was climbing into the bed above him. He looked up, but there was <u>no one</u> there. Then the crew said that they kept seeing a shadowy figure up on deck, particularly when the weather was <u>bad</u>. In the end, the captain decided to ask a priest to help. The priest said that he felt that the problem was that the dead sailor had never been buried, because he had died at <u>sea</u>, and therefore his spirit was still wandering about. So the priest came to the ship and said some prayers. He <u>prayed</u> that the dead sailor would find peace—and after that the ship had no more <u>problems</u>. But I don't know if I would like to work on it, do you?

(Adapted from *Strange but True? Casebook* by Jenny Randles)

PROCEDURE

1 Tell the students that they are going to hear a story about a ship, but that unfortunately you have a sore throat and they might not be able to hear some words. When this happens, they must either ask you politely to repeat, for example, 'Excuse me, could you say the last few words again?', or, if they think they have guessed the word, they can say, 'Excuse me, was the missing word … (sea)?' Tell the students that everybody in the

class must try to interrupt at least once. Get them to practise asking the questions.

2 Read out the text, muttering inaudibly or coughing on the words you want to obscure and then carrying on. The students should interrupt you when they cannot hear a word. They may need encouraging to begin with, but will soon enter into the spirit of the activity. If they cannot guess the word, you can encourage them to keep guessing by repeating the last few words as requested, but this time giving the first sound of the word before you have your coughing fit.

COMMENTS

1 The students usually find this activity amusing, but it does also get over the serious point that you can ask people to repeat when you do not understand something they have said.

2 Health warning to the teacher: this activity can be somewhat hard on the voice, and you may prefer muttering to coughing!

FOLLOW-UP

The students could take a text from a reader or their coursebook and do this activity in pairs, with one student reading out the text to the other student and obscuring certain words.

1.7 Over to you

LEVEL

Intermediate and above

Mrs. Snell

TIME

20 minutes

AIMS

To show students how they can control the tape recorder or video; to give students confidence in asking for clarification; to diagnose listening problems.

MATERIALS

Tape recorder or video player

PREPARATION

Choose a short listening or video passage about 3–4 minutes long which gives information about a particular topic. Documentaries, talks, phone-ins, and exam practice listening material are useful sources for this kind of text.

PROCEDURE

1 Tell the students briefly about the topic of the passage they are going to hear, for example, 'You are going to hear an interview on the radio in which a woman tells listeners about some of the jobs that are available in their area'.

2 Ask the students to suggest five questions they hope to hear answered when they listen. Write the questions on the board.

3 Ask for a student volunteer who will stop and replay the tape when the other students ask for it.

4 Ask the students to listen with their eyes closed. Explain that

this will help them to concentrate better; it will also mean that they are not affected by what other people think.

5 Tell them that if they do not understand something while they are listening, they should put their hands up. Promise that when the volunteer sees two or more hands go up, he or she will stop and replay the tape at that point as many times as necessary.

6 The students listen and try to find the answers to the questions they have devised.

7 Discuss the answers to the questions. Which questions were answered, and what were the answers? Were there some questions which were not answered? Would the recording have been more interesting if they had been answered? What do the class think the answers would have been?

COMMENTS

1 By allowing the students to control the machine, you will be able to diagnose very clearly what they find difficult in the listening passage.

2 Closing their eyes, in addition to helping them to concentrate, also stops them feeling self-conscious about putting their hands up to stop the tape.

FOLLOW-UP

After the activity is over, you might like to go back to the places in the tape that the students found difficult and analyse what the problems were. See also Activity 1. 8, 'What went wrong?'.

Acknowledgements
I first saw Sue Sheerin demonstrate this activity.

1.8 What went wrong?

LEVEL

All

TIME

15–20 minutes

AIMS

To analyse listening problems; to discuss ways of taking notes.

MATERIALS

Tape recorder

PREPARATION

Find a short listening passage (1–2 minutes) at the students' level which is fairly factual, and which contains some figures and names of people and places. Any text with a focus on giving information will do. For instance, for an advanced group, I have used excerpts from the two news summaries from *Reasons for Listening* (Scarborough 1984). Other suggestions for elementary level are 'Going ashore' from Unit 5 *Listening Elementary* (Nolasco 1987) or, for intermediate level, Unit 20, 'Places I know—Tokyo' from *Soundings* (Bell 1989) (see the Bibliography for details). Copies of the transcript will also be helpful.

PROCEDURE

1 Tell the students that they are going to hear a recording once only and that they are then going to write a summary of what they hear. They should take notes while they listen.

2 Play the recording once while the students take notes.

3 Give them about 3–4 minutes to write their summary, using their notes to help them.

4 Now play the tape again (twice if the students want you to) and ask them to make a note of any information they missed out, or got wrong.

5 With the whole class, decide which were the important points in the listening passage. In their opinion, were some of the pieces of information that they missed out not very important anyway? Draw up a list of the main points which the class feel should have been included in their summaries.

6 Elicit and write up on the board some of the problems the students had in listening and note-taking, and try to add a reason why the class think the problem happened. These are some problems and possible reasons produced by one of my classes who did this activity:

PROBLEM: difficulty in hearing or knowing how to spell people's names or place names, especially if they are foreign.

REASON: lack of geographical or political knowledge.

PROBLEM: some information missed out.

REASONS: it did not seem very important, and it was said more quietly or with falling intonation.

PROBLEM: figures misheard, for example, sixteen and sixty.

REASON: difficulty in distinguishing individual sounds.

PROBLEM: the beginning of the passage was understood better than later bits.

REASON: the listener got overloaded or tried to remember too much detail.

PROBLEM: it was impossible to make out some words or phrases at all.

REASON: they were words the students had never heard before, or they were words that were familiar, but not in their reduced form.

PROBLEM: some figures were transposed, for example, 'a march lasting 3 hours and stretching 2 miles' instead of 'a march lasting 2 hours and stretching 3 miles'.

REASON: something to do with the way we remember things?

FOLLOW-UP

1 Ask the students, in pairs, to compare the notes they took when they first listened and to come up with a suggestion about improving their note-taking. Write up the suggestions on the board.

2 Give the students the transcript so that they can also check their summaries from this.

1.9 Sight and sound 1

LEVEL

Intermediate and above

TIME

40–50 minutes

AIMS

To show how sound and vision both play a part in understanding a spoken text.

MATERIALS

Television and video.

PREPARATION

Find a short video clip (2–3 minutes) in which there is a comparatively small amount of spoken soundtrack in relation to the number of visual images. Documentaries, wildlife, and travel programmes are usually good sources of material.

PROCEDURE

1 Play the soundtrack without the visuals that go with it. You can blank out the vision either by turning down the brightness and contrast controls on the television set, or by draping something, such as a coat, over the screen. The first time they listen, the students should concentrate on getting a general idea of what the programme is about. You may like to point out that the students are experiencing the programme in much the same way that a blind person would.

2 The students get into pairs and compare what they understood. Ask for feedback to make sure that everybody understands the main points on the soundtrack. Play it again if necessary.

3 Ask the students to listen to the soundtrack once again without the vision, but this time they should individually note down the visuals which they think should accompany each stage of the soundtrack. You will probably need to stop the video three or four times to allow the students time to think and write.

4 In pairs, the students compare the visuals they suggested and discuss any differences.

5 Finally, show the video with the vision on and ask the students to compare the visuals they suggested with the ones actually chosen by the programme makers.

COMMENTS

The students will probably find that they tended to choose visuals which repeated what was said on the soundtrack. Programme makers, on the other hand, usually select a visual which, rather than mirroring what is said, extends its meaning or message in some way. The students might like to discuss the additional information which was given by the visuals in the video they saw. Sometimes programme makers will choose a visual which is completely irrelevant and which does not help people to understand the soundtrack. Ask the students if they think the visuals in the video were well chosen or not, and if there were any they would change.

1.10 Sight and sound 2

LEVEL

Intermediate and above

TIME

30 minutes

AIMS

To show how sound and vision both play a part in understanding a spoken text.

MATERIALS

The advertisement on the next page, plus a further 1–2-minute clip from the same video that you used in Activity 1.9.

PROCEDURE

1 Show the students the job advertisement for the television researcher and explain that this was a genuine job which was advertised in a British newspaper. Ask them to skim-read the advertisement and to get an impression of what the job entails. Elicit or explain that it involves writing specially designed soundtracks for television programmes so that blind or sight-impaired viewers will not lose the information in a programme which is provided by the visuals.

2 Show the video clip with both vision and sound. Check that the students have understood the general idea of what the passage is about.

3 Play the video with sound only, and ask the students, in pairs, to choose three points in the programme where they feel a non-sighted person would miss a lot of information through not being able to see the visuals. The students may like to see the clip a third time with both sound and vision to help them decide—ask them if they would like you to do this.

4 The pairs should now write two or three lines of soundtrack to compensate for these points.

5 Ask the pairs to compare the points in the programme they chose with those selected by other students. Were they the same or not? Do they think the researcher's job would be an easy one?

Researcher

Enhancing the quality of television for the blind

Central London

One of the major challenges facing television broadcasting today is finding ways to enhance viewing enjoyment for the blind and partially sighted. The TV Association – in conjunction with the Independent Television Commission, RNIB, Manchester University and electronics manufacturers – is meeting this challenge with a pioneering research programme.

Liaising closely with technical and academic teams, you will research the programme aspects of providing verbal descriptions (fitted between dialogue and carried on a separate sound channel) of the action and settings in documentary, drama, entertainment and news. Then, after extensive user testing, you will be involved in fine-tuning the results.

This is a unique opportunity for an imaginative individual to generate and progress ideas in a receptive environment.

Your background should include television production experience, preferably on programmes targeted at people with disabilities. Ideally, you will have a working knowledge of commentary production or narration, and a record of successful budget management. In addition, it would be useful if you also have experience in one or more of the following areas:

– specialist work relating to computerised voice recording

– audio visual display soundtracks

– language teaching recordings

– academic research into leisure provision for the disabled (sport or drama).

We can offer you a one-year contract, an attractive salary based on experience and ability, and the opportunity to travel within the UK.

So if you are an ideas person with energy, motivation and an understanding of the needs of people with disabilities, please contact Avril Bright, Personnel Manager, TV Association, Purbright House, 72 Corwell Street, London W10X.

1.11   Tapes for the blind

LEVEL	**Intermediate and above**
TIME	**40 minutes**
AIMS	**To follow oral instructions and seek clarification where necessary.**
MATERIALS	Tape recorders with microphones; an audio tape with instructions for blind and partially sighted people (see Step 1).

PROCEDURE

1 Explain that in Britain and probably in their country too, various bodies produce audio tapes to help blind and partially-sighted people to do things, for example:
   - cook a recipe
   - put on make-up
   - play a musical instrument
   - learn aerobics
   - learn the steps of a dance
   - find their way around a building
   - visit an exhibition.

   If you can get hold of such a tape, play a short section of it to the students. In Britain the Royal National Institute for the Blind produces a catalogue of tapes—see Appendix 2 for the address.

2 Tell the students that they are going to design a similar tape and ask them to get into groups of three or four.

3 The groups should decide which activity they would like to teach, and rehearse what they are going to say on the tape. It helps if one of them takes the role of the blind person, closes his/her eyes and tries to follow the instructions while the others speak. He or she should ask questions when the instructions are not clear.

4 When they are ready, the groups should record their instructions.

5 Play several of the tapes to the whole class, and ask them to listen with their eyes closed, and comment on the instructions from a blind person's point of view, perhaps miming the instructions as they are given on the tape. Are they clear? Are there any that could be improved? Would they be improved by adding to or reducing what is said on the tape? The class will find that problems in following the instructions usually occur because they have not said enough to make up for the fact that there is no visual element to the message.

FOLLOW-UP

The students might like to find out if charities for the blind and partially sighted in their country would like help in making such tapes, and make some for actual use.

COMMENTS

If the first attempts at recording do not come out very well, give the students the quiz at the end of Activity 7.1 (page 122) and refer to Appendix 1 (page 133).

1.12 The good listener

LEVEL	**Intermediate and above**
TIME	**30 minutes**
AIMS	**To show the students that listening is not a passive activity.**
MATERIALS	Tape recorder

PREPARATION

1 Record an excerpt from an interview or discussion from the radio or television (about 2–3 minutes) and transcribe what is said. Avoid political discussions as these are usually not good examples of co-operative listening! You could reuse some authentic material of this type that the students have listened to in an earlier class, since they will probably not have looked at it from this angle.

2 Make copies of the transcript and of the 'Good Listener' list below.

PROCEDURE

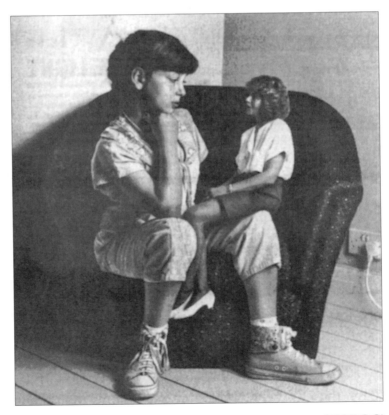

(NSPCC)

1 Show the students the picture of the adult sitting on the child's knee and tell them it featured in a national advertising campaign. Ask the students what they think the photo is trying to show, and why they think the campaign was necessary. (It was to encourage parents to listen to their children.)

2 Ask the students whether they think that children are the only people who need to be listened to. Get them to think of a person they know who is a good listener.

3 Divide the students into pairs and ask them to discuss some of the qualities which make the people they are thinking of 'good listeners'.

4 Give out the following list and ask the students whether they mentioned some of the things on it.

A good listener:

— shows he or she is interested in what the speaker is saying: by keeping eye contact, nodding, making encouraging noises, and so on

— is not distracted by other things that are going on around, but concentrates on the speaker

— is not afraid to ask the speaker to explain something he or she has not understood

— knows when the speaker wants him/her to respond or to keep quiet

— encourages the speaker to carry on if he or she hesitates

— does not keep interrupting

— does not discriminate, and listens equally carefully to men and women, children, and old people, relations and strangers, people he or she likes or does not like

— really tries to listen to what the speaker wants to say, rather than always trying to change the topic to what he or she wants to talk about

— tries to figure out not only what the speaker is saying, but why

— tries to empathize with the speaker, to the point where he or she would be able to finish a sentence for the speaker, if the speaker were suddenly lost for words

— when it is his/her turn to speak, shows he or she has been listening because he or she starts off by referring to or saying more about what the previous speaker has said

— is too good to be true, if he or she can do all these things at once!

---

5 Ask the students to listen to the excerpt you have recorded and check that they have understood broadly what is being talked about.

6 Ask the students to listen again with the transcript and to focus on one of the participants. In pairs, they should decide what they think about that participant's skill as a listener. They may like to listen more than once. They might find these questions useful:

Is he or she a good listener?
Did he or she do any of the things on the list?
How could he or she improve as a listener?
How does he or she compare as a listener with the other participants?

7 The class should share their findings.

FOLLOW-UP

The class might like to follow up this activity by practising their own listening skills. You can divide them into groups of three, consisting of two participants and one observer. Ask the two participants to do a role play or discuss a controversial topic, and ask the observer to comment on the listening skills demonstrated by the participants, after they have spoken for two or three minutes.

COMMENTS

British Telecom publishes a free book, *Talkworks*, which gives advice on how to be a good listener (see Appendix 2 for details).

1.13 Learning through listening

LEVEL

All

TIME

20 minutes for preparation plus 20 minutes for testing and feedback a week later.

AIMS

To think about ways to learn a language through listening.

MATERIALS

Some of the students will need access to a tape recorder in order to record and listen at home or in a self-access area.

The advertisement on the next page, or any similar one which claims that listening is an important aid in learning a language.

PROCEDURE

1 Show the students the advertisement on the next page. Ask them whether they agree with it. Has anybody in the class tried learning a language using this method, for instance? How successful was it? Do they think that it is a good way to learn some areas of the language but not others? If so, which ones?

(Reader's Digest)

2 Tell the students that they are going to conduct an experiment to find out if listening is a good way to remember vocabulary and structures when learning a language. In pairs, they should look over the units of their coursebook that they have covered recently, or their notes for the last few lessons, and decide on some new words, phrases, and structures which they would like to remember. This is a good opportunity for some revision!

3 Ask each pair to suggest one or more words or structures from their list and write the suggestions on the board. After the class have pooled their ideas they should choose four structures and 8–10 words which they are all going to work on.

4 Explain that some of the class are going to revise these things visually, and the others by listening to them on cassette, with the aim of finding out which seems to be the best method. Ask for volunteers who can record and listen to themselves at home. You will need a minimum of three or four volunteers and it is better if half the class can agree to be home 'listeners'. If it is difficult to find students who can record and listen at home, you might be able to arrange for a few students to do it in school. The other students will revise the items by reading them visually.

5 Explain to the class that they will remember the items better by contextualizing them, and ask them (in pairs or separately) to write a dialogue or a story which includes all the words and structures which the class have decided on. When they have finished, check that they have used the items correctly.

6 Tell the class that you will test how much they remember in one of the following week's lessons—do not specify exactly which one. Decide with the class how many times the dialogue or story should be revised using their chosen method, by reading or by listening, and at what intervals. Stress that they must stick to the rules they have decided on.

7 Without warning, during one of the next week's lessons, ask the students to write down as much as they can remember of the story or dialogue, and then check it against the original. Discuss with the students whether there seems to be any difference in the performance of the two groups using the different methods of revising, and if there are any other factors which need to be taken into consideration.

COMMENTS

This of course cannot claim to be a serious scientific experiment, and the students will be able to suggest lots of other factors which may have affected the results, such as forgetting to do the revising, or writing too long a story, or being a more 'visual' or 'aural' learner. The purpose of the activity is really to show the students that they can use listening as a method of learning the language outside class.

FOLLOW-UP 1

If the students seem to like the listening method of revising, suggest they could use it for tests and exams in the future. They might also want to use it for revising pronunciation, stress and intonation. Point out that coursebooks often have accompanying tapes which they could invest in.

FOLLOW-UP 2

If you do not mind students recording your lessons, discuss which parts might be the most useful to record and listen to at home (for example, introducing new vocabulary or structures, or pronunciation practice).

1.14 Design your own listening course

LEVEL

Elementary and above

TIME

5–10 minutes in class; 10 minutes a day for a week outside class; 10–15 minutes' feedback in class.

AIMS

To focus on different types of listening, listening problems, and the students' listening needs; to give the students some say in the kind of listening they practise in class.

PROCEDURE

1 Explain to the students that with your help they are going to design a short listening course which will be tailor-made to suit their needs.

2 Ask the students to keep a 'listening diary' over a period of a week. In this they should try to record at least seven occasions when they have listened to something in English. For each listening event they should make notes on the questions below.

Listening Diary

1 What kind of listening was it? For example, news on the radio, a song, people talking, a film, a lecture?

2 How many people were speaking?

3 Why were you listening?

4 Were you successful at listening?

5 If you were not successful, what were the problems? How did you try to solve them?

Photocopiable © Oxford University Press

3 After a week, ask the students to compare their listening diaries. Hold a class discussion about the most popular or common types of listening, any problems people experienced, and what strategies they used to try and overcome them.

4 Each student should then note down two types of listening that he or she would like to practise more.

5 Ask the students for feedback, and write up the types of listening mentioned on the board.

6 With the students decide which the most frequently mentioned types of listening seem to be. Which are going to be the most useful for learning English? Decide:
   – how much time should be spent on listening in the next few classes
   – what types of listening the class should concentrate on
   – what order they should be done in.

VARIATION

For Step 2, instead of keeping the diary over a week, at the beginning of the lesson ask the students to think back over the past week and note down the details of four listening events.

COMMENTS

If you have a low-level monolingual class, you could conduct this activity in their mother tongue.

FOLLOW-UP

As the teacher, you are now responsible for looking through the commercial listening material you have available and the other possibilities you have to hand, and choosing listening practice materials and activities which will fit into the framework which the students have devised. In the following few weeks, do activities based on this framework. Several of the ideas in this book may help you in this.

1.15 Taped feedback

LEVEL **Intermediate and above**

TIME **30 minutes outside class for the students, then about 10 minutes outside class for the teacher, then a further 15 minutes outside class for the students.**

AIMS **To show the students how they can use listening as a way of improving their speaking skills.**

MATERIALS Tape recorders

PROCEDURE 1 Ask a few students at a time to record themselves, either at home or using a tape recorder at school, speaking on a topic of their own choice for about two minutes. They can make notes beforehand to help them, if they like, but when they speak on the tape, they should speak as freely as possible, and just use their notes to refer to. Point out that they can use the pause button on the tape recorder if they need to stop and collect their thoughts at any point.

2 Before they hand over the tapes to you, each student should listen carefully to the tape he or she has made and add a short section at the end of the tape mentioning any mistakes he or she has noticed.

3 Listen to the tapes and write a short comment on the content of the talk— perhaps a question you would like to ask. Then write down some of the mistakes in pronunciation, grammar, or vocabulary which you hear. You should not attempt to note down all the errors, but just a sample of the most noticeable ones. You should spend no more than 10 minutes on each tape.

4 Return the tape to the students, together with your comments.

5 The students should read your comments and then replay their tapes, pressing the pause button when they hear a mistake, and correcting it out loud.

COMMENTS 1 If you have a big class, you will probably not want to listen to 40 tapes all at once, so you might like to have a few students do this activity per week.

2 This activity could be used as a means of giving an end of year mark for oral performance.

VARIATION John Green and Liz Lara (TESL-L e-mail contributors) have used audio tapes to comment on their students' written work, either by reading the students' work aloud on to the tape and rephrasing where the student has made a mistake, or by commenting on individual errors. They point out that if you comment on individual errors, it is essential to get the students to number the lines in their work. The students seem to appreciate this feedback, and pay more attention to it than to written comments on their work.

FOLLOW-UP   The students might like to donate a corrected version of their tape to a class or school tape library (see Activity 2.9).

Acknowledgements

This idea was inspired by an article by Diana Allan in *ELT Journal*, Vol. 45/1.

1.16 Listening outside class

LEVEL   **Intermediate and above**

TIME   **5–10 minutes**

AIMS   **To encourage the students to think of ways they can practise listening outside class.**

PROCEDURE   1 Write these unfinished sentences on the board, or dictate them to the students:

---

1 Send a cassette of yourself speaking in English to …
2 Watch …
3 Phone up …
4 Ask the teacher to record you …
5 Listen regularly to …
6 Give a blank cassette to your teacher when …
7 Use the Internet to …

---

2 Give the students the unfinished sentences and tell them that these are all suggestions for things they can do outside class to improve their listening skills. Unfortunately, the second half of each sentence has been lost.

3 In pairs, ask them to complete the sentences in any way they like.

4 After about 5 minutes, pool the suggestions (see below for some ideas from my students). Ask the students if they can add any further ideas for ways of practising listening outside class.

CASSETTE POST

CASSETTE POST

If you've got friends or family faraway, there's nothing nicer than hearing the
sound of their voice. So how's this for a great idea? 15 minutes worth of
uninterrupted chat on your own personal cassette.
With Cassette Post you can record your own message and send it almost
anywhere in the world in a special padded envelope for just £2.25.
And there's a return address label so watch the post,
and see who answers you back.

(Irish General Post Office)

VARIATION

Mix up the 'Suggested answers' and give them to the students at Step 1 with the unfinished sentences. Ask them to fit the questions and answers together as a matching exercise. This will act as a warm-up and help them think of some ideas of their own.

Suggested answers

1 … a friend instead of a letter. Ask him/her to send you one back (in English!)

2 … television, films, etc. in English.

3 … a friend, but talk in English.

4 … speaking in English. He or she could listen to it, and write down some of your errors. You could then listen to yourself, with the teacher's notes, and notice your errors.

5 … radio programmes in English.

6 … you hand in a piece of written work. The teacher could record his/her comments, instead of writing them on your work.

… you would like him/her to record part of the lesson or lecture for you to listen to afterwards.

7 … find lyrics of songs, and then listen to them with the words (some groups put lyrics on their fan page on the Net).
… use RealAudio to talk to people, or listen to radio stations such as CBS.

2 Helping students to create their own listening texts and tasks

The activities in this chapter are designed to make the students' experiences of listening in a class, irrespective of their current level of English, ones that build confidence, provide motivation, entertain, and generally make listening a less stressful activity. This is done by personalizing the listening the students do. Instead of listening to material which has been recorded outside the classroom at another time and place, and which may as a result seem rather remote to the students, they are shown ways of making their own listening texts and tasks, using their own voices or those of people they know, such as the teachers in the school, and deciding on their own goals and reasons for listening. This will mean that they are listening to familiar voices, and to topics that will interest and motivate them.

There has been some discussion over the last few years of the ways in which 'teacher talk' could be used in the classroom, and some of the activities in this Chapter (2.7, 2.8, 2.9, and 2.10), as well as some activities in Chapters 1 and 3 (1.5, 1.6, 3.4, 3.11), suggest ways in which teachers could use their own voices as sources of listening material for their students. This is an area which is worth developing and for which you will probably have lots of ideas of your own. When the students are able to listen to a speaker whom they can see or interact with, they become active participants in the listening process rather than passive overhearers, the latter unfortunately being a role they are often placed in by pre-recorded listening material.

Because the idea of making their own listening texts and tasks may be fairly new to many students, the listening texts in this chapter are quite short (perhaps even just sounds) and many of the suggested tasks are quite easy too—such as matching pictures, drawing, and making a physical response. The tapes which the students make could be put in a school 'tape library' so that other classes could listen to them. It is a good idea to do this kind of listening practice, which encourages the students to interact with and 'own' the listening they do, before going on to listening material in the coursebook, (Chapter 4) or real-life listening (Chapters 4, 5, 6, and 7), over which they will have less control. Appendix 1 contains advice on making recordings.

Students making their own recordings

2.1 Soundtracks

LEVEL

Elementary and above

TIME

50 minutes

AIMS

To follow oral instructions; to listen for details; to show students how to make their own listening materials and design tasks to go with them.

MATERIALS

You will need to provide 10 to 20 postcards or photographs showing different places in the town or city where the class is taking place. There should be enough for each student or pair of students to have a different picture. (Alternatively, the students could go on a class walk and take their own photographs or slides.) You will also need a tape recorder for the students to record themselves.

PROCEDURE

1 Tell the class that they are going to record a commentary—it could be for a tourist bus going round their town, or for a tape you could rent from the tourist office which enables you to do your own tour on foot while listening to a commentary. Show the class one of the postcards or photographs. By asking simple questions, and giving help with the answers, show them how they can build up a description of the place they can see in the picture:

What is it?	*It is a castle/stadium/park …*
What's it like?	*It looks old/new/ugly …*
	It has a tower/museum …
	There is a river/there are some swans …
Where is it?	*It's near/opposite …*
How do you get there?	*You go past the information office …*

2 Hand out the other pictures so that each student or pair of students has a different one.

3 Ask the students to write a description of their picture following the model you have given them in Step 1.

4 Check the descriptions for language mistakes and ask the students to make any corrections that are necessary. Then ask the class to discuss the order in which they are going to talk about the pictures (it should follow the route a bus or a walker on foot would take). Suggest some simple ways of linking one picture with another, for example, *'next we have …' 'near to it is …' 'another nice place is …'*

5 The students take it in turns to record their commentary.

6 The class listen to the recording and make any improvements they think necessary, such as asking someone to speak more slowly or clearly.

7 The class should send the soundtrack, and pictures to another class of a similar level, who have to listen and put the pictures into the order in which they hear them on the soundtrack.

VARIATION 1
Instead of putting pictures in order, the class could devise another task for the receivers of the tape to do, such as marking a map, or answering true/false questions.

VARIATION 2
The second class could use a portable tape recorder to actually go on the walk and check if the details on the soundtrack are accurate (perhaps the first class could build in a few deliberate errors which they have to try and spot!).

VARIATION 3
Two classes could be given the same pictures and task. The two classes can then compare the recordings they make.

VARIATION 4
The second class could listen to the soundtrack without seeing the accompanying pictures, and use the recording as a set of instructions for going out to take their own photographs or slides to go with the recording. If it is difficult to take the students out, they could just make a list of photos they would have taken.

VARIATION 5
The second class could give suggestions for improving the commentary by adding to it or changing it.

VARIATION 6
Instead of a tour of the town, the students could do a tour and soundtrack of the local zoo, art gallery, or museum.

VARIATION 7
Instead of sending the tape to another class, divide the class in half. Each half can prepare a tape for the other half.

COMMENTS
If the first attempts at recording do not come out well, give the students the quiz at the end of 7.1 (page 122) and refer to Appendix 1 (page 133).

Acknowledgements
The idea for this activity was suggested to me by Verri Toste.

2.2 My home

LEVEL	**Lower-intermediate and above**
TIME	**10–20 minutes outside class, 15 minutes in class**
AIMS	**To follow oral instructions; to listen for information and detail; to show students how to make their own listening texts and design tasks to go with them.**
MATERIALS	Portable tape recorder(s).

PREPARATION

Ask for two or three volunteers who will walk round and record a 'tour' of their home, mentioning the rooms and the position of one or two pieces of furniture in each room as they pass them. The recording should last about two minutes. They should also draw a plan of their home, but without naming any of the rooms or marking in the position of any of the furniture. Make copies of the plans.

PROCEDURE

1 Give the class copies of the plans.
2 Play the students' tapes one by one. For each tape, the students should write the names of the rooms and draw in any furniture which is mentioned on the tape, and then compare their answers in pairs.
3 The students check with the person who made the tape that they got the right answers. They might also like to discuss which plan was the easiest to complete and why.
4 In pairs, each student describes the layout of their own home while their partner draws the plan for it.

2.3 Sounds of my day

LEVEL	**Intermediate and above**
TIME	**10–15 minutes in class, 1 hour outside class, then about 20 minutes in class.**
AIMS	**To listen for detail; to listen for information and detail; to show students how to make their own listening texts and design tasks to go with them.**
MATERIALS	Portable tape recorder(s).

PREPARATION

Record your own sound diary, or if this is not possible draw up a list of sounds you would use if you were recording part of a typical day in your life. For example, getting up in the morning might include: birds singing, an alarm clock, running water, water boiling or a kettle whistling, radio, letters plopping through the letterbox, shouting goodbye, door closing, starting the car or the sound of people talking and waiting for the bus, and so on.

PROCEDURE

1 Explain that you would like the students to record a 'sound diary' for a short period in their day, which will include sounds they would hear during that time.

2 Play your own tape and ask the students to identify the sounds and what time of day they are happening, or alternatively, describe what you would put in the tape.

3 Ask the students to write down some of the sounds they would include in their diary, and to compare their list with another student.

4 The students record their tapes. They may find it easier to do the recording on a day when they do not have to go to work or school. Limit the number of sounds to a maximum of 10–12. Ask the students to bring their tapes to the next class.

5 The students exchange tapes, and listen to the tape at home and try to identify the sounds and the time of day. In the next lesson, they check with their partners that they guessed correctly. Alternatively, play a few of the tapes in class, and ask the students to guess what the sounds are.

FOLLOW-UP

1 If the students like this task, they could do a sound diary of an excerpt from an unusual day, for example, a school outing or a wedding.

2 The tapes from this activity, plus a 'key' to explain the sounds, could be put in the tape library (see 2.12) for other students to listen to.

2.4 Fun with sound effects

LEVEL

All

TIME

20 minutes in class to get the students started, 20 minutes at home, 20 minutes in the next lesson

AIMS

To remove some of the stress from listening; to identify sounds; to show students how to make their own listening material.

MATERIALS

Portable tape recorder(s).

PREPARATION

Record five sound effects of your own (or you can probably find tapes of sound effects at your local library). You could also use the tape from Maley and Duff's *Sounds Intriguing*. If you want to experiment with some amateur ones which will make the students laugh, you can act out your own. See the comments at the end of this activity.

PROCEDURE

1 Play or act out your five sounds and ask the students to identify what they are.
2 Ask the students, in pairs or groups, to construct a story which will include all the sound effects.
3 Ask some of the students to tell their story, including the sound effects.
4 Ask the students to record their own five sound effects out of class. These could be:
   − unusual sound effects
   − ones telling a story
   − on a particular theme, for example, transport, horror, the weather
   − from a particular place, for example, the beach, the countryside.
5 The students bring their sound effects to the next class and ask their classmates to identify them.

COMMENTS

The following methods could be used to produce sound effects:
− glove in talcum powder or icing sugar = people walking in the snow
− leather glove flapping = birds, washing flapping in the wind
− crumpling crisp packet = fire
− clicking tongue against roof of mouth = horses
− zizz-zizz-zizz sound with mouth = drill, bee
− wib-wob-wib-wob sound with mouth = motorboat engine.

2.5 Designing a 'self help' tape

LEVEL

Intermediate and above

TIME

20–30 minutes

AIMS

To integrate listening with the other three skills.

MATERIALS

An audio tape, either in English or the students' own language, which tries to persuade people to give up smoking, control stress or insomnia, or lose weight. Tape recorder (optional).

PROCEDURE

1 Find out the opinions of the class about the topic of the tape. For example, if it is on how to give up smoking, you could ask:
   − Do any of them smoke?
   − How many people have tried a cigarette at some time in their life?

- Has anybody recently given up smoking?
- Was it difficult to do?
- How did they do it?

Elicit or tell the class that one method that seems to be popular in some countries is to use an audio tape to help convince you to give up smoking.

2 Play about 3–5 minutes of the 'self help' tape and ask the students to note down the various techniques used. Did they include:

- medical arguments from doctors on the evil effects of smoking?
- interviews with people about how they managed to give up smoking?
- soothing music?
- tips about how to give up?
- hypnosis techniques?
- anything else?

3 Ask the students to rate the effectiveness of the various techniques used. Can they think of any others? Do they think such a tape could actually help people give up smoking?

4 Ask the class to decide on a topic they would like to make a 'self help' tape for. Help them by giving the list of topics in 'Materials' above. Divide the students into groups of three or four and ask them to plan what they would put on the tape.

5 Ask the students to pool their ideas.

6 They plan and write the script for their tape.

FOLLOW-UP   The students could make the tape and put it in the 'tape library' (see 2.12).

2.6 Serial story

LEVEL   **Elementary and above**

TIME   **10–15 minutes**

AIMS   **To raise awareness of pronunciation problems; to show students how to make their own listening material.**

MATERIALS   You will need a tape recorder and a blank tape to record the students' voices.

PREPARATION   Find a joke or an anecdote, write it down in language which is at the students' level, and then split it into six or seven short parts, consisting of roughly a sentence each. Write each part on a separate piece of paper.

PROCEDURE

1 Ask for volunteers, and give each of them a slip of paper with one part of the joke or anecdote.

2 Set the rest of the class some work for five minutes, while you take the volunteers out of class into the corridor to record their part of the story (alternatively, make the volunteers responsible for organizing the recording). They should record the parts of the story in jumbled order.

3 Play the recording to the whole class. The students write down what they hear on the tape word for word, and then compare what they have written with another student. Play the tape as many times as the students want.

4 In pairs, the students put the story into the correct order. Check the answers, and discuss any problems the students had in understanding what was said on the tape.

Examples

Here is a story I have used with a lower-intermediate class:

Once upon a time a white horse walked into a bar in New York.
He asked the barman for a lemonade.
The barman was very surprised that a horse could talk, but he poured him a lemonade.
'That will be $20, please', he said to the horse.
The horse gave him the money and started to drink the lemonade
The barman watched him and finally got up the courage to say, 'We've never had a talking horse in here before'.
'With prices like yours, I'm not surprised', replied the horse.

This joke could be used with an upper-intermediate group:

Once upon a time, a reporter was sent to cover a big fire in California.
He desperately wanted to get some photographs of the fire, but, because of the heat and smoke, he could not get close enough.
Suddenly, he had a brilliant idea. He would hire a plane and fly over the fire to take his photographs.
He rang up the local airport, and booked a small plane. Then he rushed to the airport as fast as he could.
He found a small plane waiting on the runway with somebody already sitting in the pilot's seat.
He climbed into the plane and told the pilot to take off.
When they were in the air, he told the pilot to fly over the fire so that he could take his photographs.
The pilot looked very surprised and said, 'But aren't you my flying instructor?'

Photocopiable © Oxford University Press

VARIATION

If you have two rooms and two tape recorders available, split the class into two and have them make tapes for each other.

Acknowledgements
I would like to thank my former colleagues, Anne Lawrie and John Higgins, for ideas for this activity.

Using teachers' voices

2.7 Gossips

LEVEL

All

TIME

5–10 minutes

AIMS

To listen to familiar voices (members of staff in the school); to listen for detail.

PREPARATION

Ask another member of staff in the school who can speak English if he or she could come in for a few minutes during one of your lessons. He or she is going to burst into the classroom and tell the class about something dramatic that has just happened to them, for example, they have just had their purse or wallet stolen and they caught sight of the thief running away, or they have just heard that they have had a big win in the national lottery. They can include a few unbelievable elements to make it more dramatic. They should prepare what to say: they will need to speak non-stop for one or two minutes. Arrange a time when they will burst into the classroom.

PROCEDURE

1 At the beginning of the lesson, warn the class that someone may come in and that they should listen very carefully and try to remember as much as they can of what the person tells them.

2 At the time you have pre-arranged, the member of staff bursts dramatically into the classroom, tells their story, and leaves just as dramatically.

3 In pairs, the students compare what they understood and remember from what the person told them.

4 Ask the whole class to pool all the information they can remember. Do they believe everything they heard? Is there anything which seems impossible?

VARIATION

If you can get hold of two members of staff to come into the classroom, you could ask them to prepare some highly improbable (but non-malicious!) gossip about the school, students, or members of staff, instead of the dramatic story.

2.8 Describe and draw rooms from stories

LEVEL

All

TIME

20 minutes

AIMS

To listen to a familiar voice (the teacher's); to listen for detail and make a response.

PREPARATION

1 Choose or invent a description of a room to read out to the students. If a recording of the book is available you could use that. Here are some suggestions of rooms from literature:

Advanced
'The red room' from Chapter 2 of *Jane Eyre* by Charlotte Brontë.
'Miss Haversham's room' from Chapter 8 of *Great Expectations* by Charles Dickens.

Intermediate
'The doctor's room' from Chapter 1 of *The Pearl* by John Steinbeck.
'Jo's room' from *Dublin People* by Maeve Binchy, pages 8–9, Oxford Bookworms Black Series, Level 6.

Elementary
'Miss Stoner's room' from *The Speckled Band* by Sir Arthur Conan Doyle in the Oxford Bookworms Black Series, Level 2.

2 Draw your own impression of the room (optional).

PROCEDURE

1 Tell the students you are going to read them a description of a room, and that you want them to draw it afterwards. Ask them to listen for a general impression of the room first.

2 Read the description of the room to the students.

3 Elicit the students' impressions of the room. Is it big or small? Does it belong to a rich or poor person? What kind of feeling do they get about the room? Explain/elicit the meaning of any vocabulary which the students do not know.

4 Tell the students that you now want them to draw the room. Read the description again as many times as they want while they draw.

5 Ask the students to compare their drawing with the person next to them. You could also show them what your drawing would be like.

6 Discuss what the room shows about the personality of the person or people who furnished it, and the part they think it might play in the story. Ask the students if they would like to live in this room.

FOLLOW-UP   If you have access to a video of the novel or short story, you can show the students how the director visualized the room, and get their comments.

VARIATION   You can also use this activity with descriptions of people in novels and short stories.

COMMENTS   This is basically a variation on the old favourite 'describe and draw' but with the added bonus that it can be used as a way into a novel or short story or as an exercise you can use while the class are reading a set book.

2.9 Imagining

LEVEL   Lower-intermediate

TIME   5–10 minutes

AIMS   **To listen to a familiar voice (the teacher's); to listen for detail and make a response.**

MATERIALS   The beginning of a story which the students are going to finish. A picture of a scene which you can describe and use as the setting for the story. One very useful source of pictures is Maley and Duff and Grellet's (1988) *The Mind's Eye*. For my example I used a beach scene:

PROCEDURE

1 Ask the students their opinions on the topic of the story. The example here is set on a beach, so you can ask:
   - What are the good and bad things about it?
   - What is their favourite time of day or favourite season to go there?
   - What can you do there?

2 Tell the students that you are going to tell them a story which they are going to finish. Suggest that closing their eyes may help them to concentrate better.

3 Read the following story slowly to the students:

   … It is a very hot, late afternoon at the seaside, and the sun is beating down. Most people have gone home, and you have got the beach to yourself. All you can hear is the gentle sound of the sea lapping over the sand, and some sea-birds calling. Nothing and nobody for miles and miles except you, the sea, the sun, and the sand … Suddenly, you catch sight of something on the sea, a long way out to sea. You look very hard but you cannot quite see what it is. You look harder. It comes closer to you, and you can see that it is a speedboat, with two people in it. At that moment the sun suddenly goes behind a cloud, and you start to feel cold. You feel a strange sense of fear creeping over you …

4 The students write the end of the story. They could then read it out to another student.

Students designing their own tasks

2.10 Listening in role

LEVEL

Intermediate and above

TIME

30 minutes

AIMS

To give the students the experience of choosing their own reasons for listening; to show that individuals attend to and remember different things depending on their reason for listening.

MATERIALS

A tape recorder.

PREPARATION

Choose a listening text which will allow the students to listen in different roles. An item of news from the radio would be ideal for higher-level classes. You could also use your own voice and read out, for instance, an eyewitness account of an event. I used the article on the next page which a student officer wrote for a university newsletter about the San Francisco earthquake of 1989.

Then, on the 5th day it all happened! In the midst of the busy schedule of meetings, lectures and company presentations, the earth shook and San Francisco had its biggest earthquake since 1906. I find no shame in admitting that despite my previous adventures in my short but exciting life, I was absolutely terrified. In down-town San Francisco the earth shook, the buildings swayed visibly from side to side and ripples of shock waves went down the roadway as if a stone had been thrown into a still pond.

I have nothing but praise for San Franciscans. As everything started falling off the shelves of the shop I had entered – to purchase a cold drink to accompany my viewing of the World Series Baseball game – everybody around about me remained calm. 15 seconds is a long time when nature takes over, when there is an indescribable and very ominous rumbling amidst the otherwise complete silence, when windows are popping out and when bits are falling off buildings. There was no screaming or panic at all by those around me.

After the quake itself was over, people were visibly shocked. I was very conscious of having been present at a very important event. People stood around in the street in the gathering gloom just talking to strangers, glad to be alive, and fully appreciative of the fact that it could have been a great deal worse.

In the city centre there was no power, telephones or water for 2 days, a feature that was a minor consideration when it became known that the Nimitz Highway had collapsed, the Bay Bridge had been severely damaged and the Marina district had suffered a major fire.

Most unnerving of all were the after-shocks. Several of them were at least 5 on the Richter Scale. Suddenly the whole building would lurch and everybody would hold their breath for a moment wondering if this was the "big one".

The city returned to normal remarkably quickly. Buildings were inspected and power was restored. I managed to …

PROCEDURE

1 Tell the students that they are going to hear about an event, but that they are going to listen to it from a particular point of view. Some of them will be *seismologists* (elicit/explain what these are), some of them will be *reporters* (they should decide what kind of publication they are writing for), and some of them will be the girl's *mother* or *father*. Ask them to choose a role. If possible, there should be roughly equal numbers of seismologists, parents, and reporters.

2 The students listen to the account, and make notes of what interests them in their role.

3 The students compare the notes they took with those taken by somebody who was listening in another role. The notes will usually be very different. Encourage the students to think about how factors such as emotional involvement or scientific interest can affect what is noticed and remembered.

4 Put the students together with others who listened in the same role and ask them to pool their notes. Even here there will be individual differences which can be discussed, especially between the reporters, who will probably be writing for several different types of readers.

5 Finally, the seismologists could write a report on the earthquake for a geographical magazine, the reporters could interview another eye-witness of the earthquake, and the parents could role-play a telephone call to their daughter.

2.11 Guest speaker

LEVEL

Lower-intermediate and above

TIME

5 minutes in one lesson, 20 minutes in the next lesson, 50 minutes in a subsequent lesson.

AIMS

To listen for gist and details; to give the students the experience of listening as an audience (rather than as participants or overhearers).

PREPARATION

1 With the students, identify a possible guest speaker who is willing to come and talk to them for about 20 minutes. It could be one of the other teachers, or an English speaker who lives in the town, or perhaps a visitor or a student with fairly good English.

2 Ask the speaker to write a brief CV for the class, giving a few details about what they have done in their life, any famous people they have met, hobbies, interesting places they have been to, and so on. For fun, the speaker could invent a completely fictitious CV, for example, *1978–1980: astronaut, completed two trips to the moon.*

3 Make copies of the CV for the students.

PROCEDURE

1 Hand out copies of the CV to the class, put the students in pairs, and ask each pair to suggest one question they would like the guest speaker to answer. Pool the questions and decide on the 8–10 best questions. Ask the students to copy them down.

2 With the students, decide on a list of topics for the speaker which will be most likely to produce the answers to the questions. Practise polite ways of asking questions.

3 Give the list of topics to the guest speaker. These will provide guidelines for him/her in preparing the talk. He or she, however, should not know what questions the students are expecting to be answered. It will make the talk more interesting if the speaker can illustrate it, perhaps with photographs that

can be passed around, or slides. Ask the guest speaker if he or she would mind being recorded. If he or she does not mind, you could then add the talk to your tape library—see 2.12.

4 In the next class, the speaker gives his/her talk. The students should listen to see if their questions are answered.

5 If some of the questions have not been answered in the talk, the students could ask them in a question-and-answer session with the speaker after the talk has finished.

6 After the speaker has gone, go through the questions which the students prepared and check the answers.

2.12 Tape library

LEVEL

All

TIME

30–60 minutes' preparation for the teacher; 30–40 minutes for the students outside class.

AIMS

To create a tape library; to listen to familiar voices (members of staff in the school and other students); to show students how to design their own listening texts and tasks.

MATERIALS

Tape recorder with a tape-to-tape copying facility. Tape players for the students to listen to.

PREPARATION

1 Ask some of your colleagues if they could record themselves speaking in English for 2–3 minutes. Some topics they could talk about might include:

   – a hobby, especially if it is an unusual one the students would not associate them with
   – the best or worst holiday they have ever had and why
   – a cultural misunderstanding that caused embarrassment
   – the most frightening experience they have ever had
   – a book, a film, or a painting they have really enjoyed and why
   – if they are from another country or region, the best and worst things about it in their opinion, or where they would recommend that a visitor went.

   Ask them to have a certain level of student in mind when they are making the recording, and make sure that you get recordings for a number of different levels, including beginners and elementary students. You may find that the most efficient way of getting the tapes recorded is to record people yourself.

2 Make copies of the masters, and keep them separate. Make a list of the subjects on the tapes, and make photocopies of the list to distribute in class.

PROCEDURE

1 In class, distribute copies of the list of tapes, and ask the students to choose a tape to take home to listen to for homework. Alternatively, the students could bring in their own blank cassette, clearly marked with their name, for you to copy on to (this does not take as long as you might think, using a fast copier, as the listening texts are short).

2 Give the students a fixed amount of time, perhaps until the next lesson, to listen to the tapes at home and to devise a task for the next student to do when they listen to the tape.

3 In the next class, discuss any problems and redistribute the tapes and tasks.

COMMENTS

If it is difficult for students to do this kind of individual listening at home, they could do it in a language laboratory or self-access centre at school.

VARIATION 1

Ask a group of students to prepare a tape about the school for next year's students. It could be accompanied by photos of people and places. The students could also type the script so that students who listen can read it too.

VARIATION 2

You can also add to the tape library by including tapes which have been produced as a result of other activities in this chapter and in Chapter 1, for example:

1.11	Tapes for the blind
1.15	Taped feedback
2.1	Soundtracks
2.2	My home
2.3	Sounds of my day
2.5	Designing a 'self help' tape
2.11	Guest speaker
7.1	Interview for a magazine
7.2	Voice of the people
7.3	Desert island discs backwards
7.4	Making a news broadcast
7.5	A radio play
7.6	Local radio
7.7	Oral history

Recordings of songs plus copies of the lyrics, which the students can follow as they listen, are another kind of listening text which would also be a popular addition to the tape library.

3 Micro skills

The activities in this chapter focus on the 'small bits' of listening, such as recognizing particular sounds or words in the stream of speech, identifying word and sentence stress, or recognizing and understanding the function of particular intonation patterns. These are often referred to as 'bottom–up', to distinguish them from 'top–down' listening, (in which listeners use more global clues to meaning, such as their knowledge of the topic or the way in which a particular kind of spoken text is typically organized). Of course, good listeners combine both levels of listening to help them to understand what is being said, but in teaching it is sometimes useful to focus on one of the levels in a particular class.

Recently, there has been a lot of interest in helping the students to divide the spoken message they hear into units of meaning or 'chunks', which consist of groups of words expressing one thought or idea. The 'chunk' is the same as a 'tone unit' or 'intonation group', and contains one major change of pitch. If a speaker pauses, the normal place for this to happen will be between one 'chunk' and the next. Being able to identify and process these units of meaning helps the students to understand what they hear much better; as Günther Kaltenboek (1994: 19) says, 'the organisation of a text into message units has an immediate impact on intelligibility … Students need to be shown that spoken language consists of chunks rather than isolated lexical items and complete sentences'.

Another focus of research at the moment is into the ways in which listeners separate off one word from the next in the stream of speech. In English, the most common type of word is a polysyllable with its main stress on the first syllable, and native listeners identify stress in order to decide when a new word is beginning.

In this chapter, there are a number of activities which focus on these two areas, identifying individual words in the stream of speech and 'chunking', as well as others on intonation, individual sounds, and other aspects of 'bottom–up' listening.

Individual sounds

3.1 Wall dictation

LEVEL	All
TIME	15–20 minutes
AIMS	To discriminate between similar sounds.
PREPARATION	Draw up a list of sounds which your students are having difficulty in telling apart and write them on a large sheet of paper in word lists and sentences. Make enough copies of the sheet so that there is one for every four to five students. You can get ideas from a book on pronunciation such as Baker's *Ship or Sheep?*.

Below is a sheet I prepared for a group of Polish students, who were having trouble distinguishing between /p/ and /b/, /k/ and /g/, /d/ and /t/, and /v/ and /w/. They were also having problems with /ð/ and /θ/ in all positions, and the vowels /e/ and /æ/. As you can see, it does not need to be deathless prose but should include words that the students are likely to confuse.

bag	back	bag
cab	cab	cap
paper	pepper	paper
said	said	set
vest	west	vest
packed	packed	backed

He packed the car.
Show me the bag.
He sneezed and the paper went everywhere.
It is in the back.
Can you get me the pepper?

This is the story of my life in Cork so far. I arrived on the sixth of April and I shall be here for two months. It is very wet here in the west, and my clothes are not waterproof enough. I am getting thinner because of the awful food and I feel enthusiastic at the thought of going home.

PROCEDURE

1 Divide the class into groups of four or five.
2 Stick the papers on the walls. Show each group which is 'their' paper and make sure that groups are roughly the same distance from their papers and will not get in the way of furniture or other students when they go to read them.

3 Each group should nominate three of its members as 'messengers'. The other members of the group will be 'secretaries'. Explain that at a sign from you, all the groups will send one of their messengers up to the wall to read their paper. The messengers must remember as much as they can from the paper and come back and dictate it to the group, who will copy it down. They can go to the wall as many times as they need to. The first group to correctly write everything on the sheet correctly will be the winners.

4 Explain that at intervals you will shout 'Change!' and at that point the current messenger in each group must sit down, and the next messenger must go to the wall.

5 Emphasize that messengers should walk as quickly as possible, not run, and that they must come back to the group to deliver their message, not stand at the wall and shout! The skill lies in remembering as much as possible and saying it correctly when they get back to the group. They are not allowed to spell words to the group, but if the group get the word wrong, they can repeat it again until the group get it right. (This allows for lots of listening and speaking practice of the target sounds.)

6 Do a 'practice run' of the activity, just to check that the students know what to do, before starting the activity for real.

COMMENTS

Not for small classrooms or classes of over 25 students—the furniture could get in the way!

Acknowledgements
I adapted this activity from Davis and Rinvolucri's *Dictation*.

3.2   People's sounds

LEVEL

Elementary and above

TIME

15 minutes

AIMS

To recognize particular sounds.

MATERIALS

Magazine pictures of people (non-famous), enough for one picture between two or three students.

PREPARATION

Prepare one picture yourself, by selecting a sound you want to focus on and constructing an imaginary description of job, hobbies, likes and dislikes, and so on, for the person in the picture. The sound should appear frequently in the description. For example, you could choose the sound /iː/ and your description could be something like this:

This is Tina. She is almost sixteen and she comes from Queensland in Australia. She is studying at the moment and she is not sure what job she wants to do in the future—perhaps work on a magazine or be a teacher. She likes skiing but she hates tennis and swimming. Her favourite foods are peas and ice cream and her favourite colour is light green.

PROCEDURE

1 Explain to the students that you are going to describe a person's lifestyle and you want them to guess which sound you are focusing on. Hold up your picture and describe the person in it, while the students try to guess the sound. You may have to read the description more than once.

2 Divide the students into pairs, and give each pair a picture. Ask the students to write a brief description of the lifestyle of the person in their picture, focusing on a particular sound.

3 The pairs should take it in turns to read out their descriptions while the rest of the class try to guess the sound they were focusing on.

Acknowledgements
I first saw Pat Collier do this activity.

3.3 Weird words

LEVEL

All

TIME

10 minutes

AIMS

To think about the ways in which sounds can be represented in written form.

PREPARATION

Find 10–12 words which the students will have not met before. Here is a list I prepared for a lower-intermediate class:

weight	*oxygen*	*biscuit*	*colleague*	*advertisement*
anxious	*ghost*	*whisky*	*doubt*	*nephew*

PROCEDURE

1 Explain to the students that you are going to dictate some words that they may not know. They must try to guess how the words are spelt from their sounds, and from their knowledge of English spelling.

2 The students write down the words as you dictate them. Repeat each word more than once.

3 Ask the students to get into pairs and compare how they spelt the words.

4 Give the students the answers by spelling out the words, rather than writing them on the board, to give them more listening practice. The students can give themselves one point for each word they managed to spell correctly.

5 Elicit/explain the meaning of the words and discuss any surprises—for example, that English spelling can contain letters which are not sounded, like the 'b' in 'doubt', and the fact that the same sound can be spelt in a number of ways, for example /i:/ can be spelt as 'y' or 'ea'.

6 If the students know the phonetic alphabet, they can devise in pairs a similar dictation for each other, looking up the words they use to test their partner in a dictionary which shows how the words are pronounced as well as spelt.

3.4 Discrimination quiz

LEVEL

Lower-intermediate and above

TIME

5–10 minutes

AIMS

To help students with some of the problems in understanding caused by weak forms, similar sounds, and word divisions.

PREPARATION

Make copies of the following quiz:

Discrimination quiz

Tick the one the teacher says:

1. a She wants a present.
   b She wants her present.
2. a Two pens are mine.
   b Two pens of mine …
3. a The way to serve it …
   b The waiter served it.
4. a I won't go.
   b I want to go.
5. a I lived here for ten years.
   b I've lived here for ten years.
6. a I can swim.
   b I can't swim.
7. a He'd come every day.
   b He'll come every day.
8. a He shouldn't have done it, really.
   b He should've done it, really.
9. a What was he doing?
   b What was she doing?
10. a India is a nation state.
    b India is an Asian state.

PROCEDURE

1 Give out copies of the discrimination quiz and ask the students to get into pairs and decide what the difference in meaning is between each pair of sentences.

2 Tell the students that they are going to listen and tick the right answer when you say one of the alternatives.

3 Read out one of the alternatives, a or b for each question. Do it in a relaxed and fairly brisk fashion so that students get practice in hearing the reduced forms of sounds. Be careful not to put unnatural stress on any of the words.

4 Give or elicit the answers and discuss any that the students found difficult.

FOLLOW-UP

The pairs can test each other using the same list.

Word stress

3.5 Holiday stress

LEVEL

Elementary and above

TIME

15 minutes

AIMS

To identify stressed syllables in words.

PROCEDURE

1 Remind the students about the different positions in a word where the main stress can come by writing a few words on the board, for example:

India   Japan   Australia   Britain   Spain

Get the students to help you mark the stress patterns for each of the words, by putting a large dot for the major stressed syllable and small dots for the unstressed syllables, like this:

• ● ••
Australia

2 Ask the students to decide individually which country they would really like to visit most in the whole world, given unlimited funds for travelling.

3 Get the students to mingle, telling each other where they would like to go, for example, 'I'd like to go to Spain', 'I'd like to go to the Caribbean'. Their task is to form a group with the people who want to go to countries with the same stress pattern as theirs. They will need to keep repeating the name of their country and thinking about where the main stress comes until they have collected all the others who belong in their group.

4 While the students are doing this, stick large pieces of paper on the walls, each showing a particular stress pattern, for example:

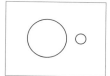    

You can also have one piece of paper which says 'anything else'.

5 When they are ready, the students go and stand by the stress pattern which they think fits the country they want to go to. The category 'anything else' will cover items like 'The Czech Republic' which do not fit the other patterns you have put up on the walls. You can ask the students in this group to help each other to draw stress patterns for the countries they have chosen.

VARIATION

You can repeat this activity by asking the students to choose their favourite in other categories besides country, for example favourite food, girls' names, animals, football teams, and so on.

Acknowledgements

I am grateful to my former colleague Cathy Gannon for this idea.

Identifying words in a stream of speech

3.6 Haunted in room 325

LEVEL

Intermediate and above

TIME

40 minutes

AIMS

To identify particular words in the stream of speech; to give the students experience in designing their own listening tasks.

PREPARATION

Find an interesting section from a story which can be cut into two roughly equal parts. For more advanced students one good source is the 'reader experience' stories from women's magazines. For lower-level students you could use a graded reader (see the Variation at the end of this activity). The story below is from a women's magazine and is suitable for upper-intermediate and advanced students.

It happened to me

'I was haunted in room 325'

For air stewardess Leonie Ball, it was a regular trip to Rome. But the eerie events made it a night she'd never forget - and one which changed her life

A

No, I've never been superstitious nor particularly interested in the paranormal. I certainly never believed in ghosts. But I'll never forget the events of the most chilling night of my life, events for which there's no explanation other than a haunting...

I was working as an air stewardess and had travelled to Rome on a late night flight from London. It was chilly, dark and wet when we were driven from the airport to stay overnight at a hotel.

It wasn't the one we normally used because that was full, but it was very grand, with high ceilings and marble columns. The ornate, rattling radiators and old lifts gave it a feeling of neglect and we joked that it was creepy. But it was welcome, as we really needed our rest. I went straight to my room.

A couple of hours later, I was woken by the most terrible screams, sobbing and shouts. It seemed to be coming from the room next door, or maybe from the street. It was the sound of a woman in awful distress, with two male voices laughing and sneering. I thought someone was being attacked.

When the screaming woman spoke, it was in Italian. The men, their voices thick and rasping, also spoke Italian, but were more guttural.

'I was woken by terrible screams'

In the end, hands shaking, I phoned reception. No, there had been no other complaints - and why should there be? After all, the room next to mine was empty. Kindly, they agreed to send porters to check the corridor. They would also bring me some milk to help me get back to sleep.

B

Then, just as I put the phone down, the noises stopped abruptly. I jumped out of bed and ran into the corridor to see if anyone was coming out of the room, but nobody appeared except two porters and a maid with my milk.

The porters went to the room next door. It was empty, the bed undisturbed. The maid calmed me down and apologised on behalf of the hotel. I felt so silly. The staff reckoned I'd probably heard a loud radio playing in the street but I was convinced of what I'd heard.

I tried to sleep for what was left of the night. I didn't even mention my experience to any of the crew, all of whom had enjoyed a perfectly peaceful night. I would have forgotten about it, I suppose, but for something the captain said as we made the return flight to London.

He'd stayed in a different hotel, because that was British Airways practice, but he knew about the place we'd stayed as a result of his wartime experiences. He joked about whether we would have been comfortable in our hotel had we known in advance that it had been used by the Gestapo during the war. Italian partisan prisoners, it was said, had been interrogated there in what were now guest bedrooms. At the time, I said nothing. But I was so shocked, later, I was physically sick.

I can't understand it. I'm sure the captain was telling the truth because his account of the hotel's history has been backed up by other sources.

'No one can explain what I heard'

And I'm sure I heard real noises that night, strange, sinister and upsetting noises. It would be convenient to think it was just a radio blaring outside a creepy old hotel, but I just can't believe that. No one can explain what I heard that night in Rome. But I know that those screams were real - as real as the marble columns, the rickety old lifts, huge key and high door to the room in the hotel I can never forget.

PROCEDURE

1 Divide the story into two roughly equal parts, **A** and **B**.

2 Divide the class into an even number of groups. Each group should contain about four or five students.

3 Give half of the groups part **A** of the text, and the other half part **B**.

4 Each group should read their part of the text and together decide on ten key words which will help them retell the story. Warn them that they will have to retell the story without looking at the text. They should write their list of words on a piece of paper in the order they will use them in the retelling. Circulate and help with any problems in reading and understanding the text.

5 Let the groups practise telling their stories, using the key words. They should decide which member of the group will tell which part of the story.

6 Tell each group that they are going to devise a test for the group who will hear their story. They should write the list of key words in jumbled order on another piece of paper.

7 Put each group who got text **A** with a group who got text **B**.

8 Each group hands over their test list of jumbled key words to the other group.

9 Starting with the group that got text **A**, each group retells their story to the other group, using their list of key words, and taking it in turns to tell parts of the story. The other group should listen for the words on their list and decide on the order they hear them in.

10 Afterwards, the two groups can compare their 'tests'. Why were some words more difficult to hear than others?

VARIATION

Instead of using a written text, you could use two sections of a graded reader on cassette. Half the class can listen to half the story on one tape recorder, while the others listen to the other half in another room.

COMMENTS

1 The instructions in this activity are complicated so you will need to stop and give the next instruction to the students after each step of the activity.

2 If the students have difficulty in reading, let them have the texts the night before.

3.7 Shouting match

LEVEL

All

TIME

10–15 minutes

AIMS

To cope with background noise.

PREPARATION   Write 5–7 phrases or short sentences on a number of cards. You can use ones which the class have recently learnt. Each card should have different sentences and there should be one card for every 4–5 students. This is an example of one I prepared for an elementary class:

> My name is Tom Cruise
> I live in Los Angeles
> My telephone number is 021–55497
> I like surfing and baseball
> I am an actor

Alternatively, let the students prepare their own cards.

PROCEDURE   1 Divide the class into an even number of groups of four to five students.
2 Explain that each group is going to work with another group, and the first pair of groups to complete their task successfully will be the winners.
3 Tell the groups which other group they will be working with.
4 Ask the groups to stand up and go to the opposite end of the classroom from the group they are working with.
5 Tell the groups that at a signal from you each group must shout out the information on their card to the other group, who must write it down correctly, and then shout back the information on their card. When the two groups have finished, they should put up their hands and you will check whether what they have written is correct. The first pair of groups who are totally accurate (including spelling) will win. The only problem is that all the other groups will be shouting to each other at the same time and they will have to listen very carefully to pick out their own information.

COMMENTS   1 This is a noisy activity, so make sure your classroom is fairly sound-proof, or warn your colleagues that there will be some noise for about five minutes!
2 If you want to lower the sound volume, you can specify that individuals in each group, rather than the whole group, take it in turn to shout out what is on the card, or that, instead of shouting, they whisper. This will, however, reduce the usefulness and fun of the activity.

Acknowledgements
I first saw Tim Murphey do this exercise, and like him, I have found it a very good way of giving confidence to students who are shy about talking.

3.8 Predictaword

LEVEL	**Lower-intermediate and above**
TIME	**10–15 minutes**
AIMS	**To listen for particular words in a stream of speech.**
PROCEDURE	1 Ask for a volunteer who will speak on a particular topic for two or three minutes. Let the class decide on the topic—it should be something fairly simple, for example, describe the room we are in, tell us about your weekend, describe your pet, tell us about your last holiday.
	2 The volunteer goes outside the room for a couple of minutes to plan what he or she is going to say.
	3 Meanwhile the class predict six words which they are sure the volunteer will say (frequently occurring functional words such as 'the', 'a', 'is', and so on are not allowed!) and six words which they think he or she might say, but are not sure.
	4 The volunteer is then called back into class and talks on the topic for two to three minutes. The other students get one point for each of the six 'sure' words the volunteer says, and two points for each of the 'less sure words' he or she says.
	5 The activity can be repeated with another volunteer.

3.9 Snakes and stars

LEVEL	**Intermediate and above**
TIME	**5–10 minutes**
AIMS	**To improve ability to listen closely to individual words.**
PREPARATION	This game can be played in pairs, or as two teams. The instructions given here are for playing the game in pairs. You will need to prepare a card with a different list of 5–6 categories on it for Student A and B in each pair. Make enough copies for each student. Some possible categories are:

Student A

things you can find in the jungle
places where you can find water
people who work above the ground, not on it
things you can find in America
people whose jobs involve danger
things made out of gold

> **Student B**
> things you can find in the sky
> electrical things you can find in a kitchen
> things you will need on holiday
> people who wear a uniform
> things you might need to survive on a desert island
> things made out of glass

Photocopiable © Oxford University Press

PROCEDURE

1 Divide the class into pairs and give out the cards. Explain that they must keep what is written on their card a secret.

2 Tell the students that the aim of the game is to guess the category that is written on their partner's card. He or she will help them to guess by giving examples of words in the category, without saying what is written on his/her card. If, for example, the category is 'things you can find in the desert', he or she can give clues like 'cactus', 'snake', or 'camels', but may not mention the word 'desert'. Give the students time to jot down some words they could say for each of the categories on their card.

3 The other student must listen until he or she thinks he or she has heard enough words to guess the category. He or she is only allowed one guess, so should wait until he or she is very sure of the category. He or she cannot ask the other student any questions, just listen, although it is permissible to ask them to repeat or spell words, and both sides are allowed to use dictionaries.

4 The students take it in turns to guess each other's categories. It is a good idea to set a time limit, for example, each student is allowed two minutes to guess their partner's category.

3.10 Wrong word quiz

LEVEL

Lower-intermediate and above

TIME

10–15 minutes

AIMS

To identify and correct words in a stream of speech.

PREPARATION

Prepare a set of sentences, with roughly two sentences per student. Each sentence should contain one word which gives wrong information, for example:

Levi-Strauss is the name of a make of jam.
Barcelona is a city in Italy.
John Gallagher sings with the group Oasis.

Ten plus six is sixty.
Spiders have six legs.

You can tailor the sentences to the students' interests, or for EAP or ESP classes, to a subject they are studying or have expertise on. You can also focus on the sounds you know they confuse, such as *sixteen* and *sixty*, *can* and *can't*, and so on. Alternatively, ask the students each to write a sentence for the opposing team and collect them in.

PROCEDURE	1 Divide the class into two teams.
	2 Read out the sentences to each team in turn. The members of the team should take it in turn to listen to and correct a sentence. They get one point if they can answer straight away, half a point if the rest of the team helps.
	3 The team with the most points at the end of the quiz wins.
COMMENTS	Instead of reading the sentences yourself, you could get the students to read them out.

Sentence stress

3.11 Audio books 1

LEVEL	**All**
TIME	**10–15 minutes**
AIMS	**To recognize words which are stressed in sentences, and to think about why they are stressed.**
MATERIALS	Tape recorder, audio book.
PREPARATION	1 There are many 'audio books' in the shops featuring a well-known actor or the author reading a novel on to an audio cassette. Find a short excerpt from an 'audio book' at the students' level (about five to six lines in the written version). For lower levels, a number of graded readers have accompanying cassettes.
	2 Type out a written version of the excerpt and make copies.
PROCEDURE	1 Give each student a copy of the written version of the excerpt and ask them to mark the words which they think the reader on the tape will stress. It will probably be helpful if they read the transcript aloud to themselves while they are doing this.
	2 Ask the students to compare their answers in pairs, and then pool the answers. Discuss why they think these particular words will be stressed. Explain/elicit the idea that it is often 'content'

words (nouns, verbs, adjectives, and adverbs) which receive stress, but that they also have to consider other things like the emotions of the characters and important events in the story.

3 Discuss with the students how they can recognize stressed syllables in stressed words. (These syllables will often be louder, slower, longer and with a noticeable change in tone/pitch.)

4 Ask the students to listen to the audio version and check if they were correct. They will probably want to listen to the recording more than once.

FOLLOW-UP

The students make a list of the words that were stressed and try to retell the story in pairs, referring only to the list.

3.12 Stresses and pauses

LEVEL

Upper-intermediate and above

TIME

20 minutes

AIMS

To recognize pauses which indicate the end of one 'chunk' of information and the beginning of another; to help the students to recognize the stressed words in an utterance.

MATERIALS

Tape recorder.

PREPARATION

1 Record about 30 seconds of a spontaneous interview or commentary from English-language television or radio (the news is not very suitable, because being scripted, it will follow some of the conventions of written language).

2 Make a transcript of what is said, but leave out any punctuation. Make a copy for each student.

PROCEDURE

1 Give each student a copy of the transcript.

2 Ask them to mark in where they would put full stops and commas if they were punctuating this as a written text.

3 Play the recording, and this time ask the students to mark the transcript with a vertical line when the speaker pauses. They will probably need to hear the recording more than once.

4 Ask the students to compare the two kinds of 'punctuation'. Were they different? (For example, speakers tend to pause at the end of a 'chunk' of information, which can be in what looks like the middle of a phrase or sentence in grammatical terms.) Why do they think the speaker paused there? Was it because he or she had finished an idea, or was planning what to say next?

5 Next, ask the students to mark the words which they think were stressed by the speaker (it will probably be helpful if they read the transcript aloud to themselves while they are doing this).
6 Play the recording again so that students can check whether they were correct.
7 Ask the students whether there seems to be any connection between the stressed words and the pauses. Does the speaker tend to pause after a stressed word?

Longer stretches of language

3.13 What's next?

LEVEL	**All**
TIME	**5 minutes**
AIMS	**To help students predict what they will hear next.**
MATERIALS	A recording at the students' level, about 1–2 minutes long. It could be one the students have already listened to in a previous lesson. A tape recorder.
PROCEDURE	1 Give the students a brief outline of what the tape is about.
2 Play (or let one of the students play) the tape and stop it at random. Ask the students to write down the next words or the next idea they think they will hear.
3 Carry on playing the tape. The students check whether they wrote down something similar to what was said on the tape. Discuss the kinds of clues they used to decide what would come next.
4 Repeat this activity about ten times, continuing through the tape.

Intonation

3.14 Kind or cruel?

LEVEL	**All**
TIME	**10–15 minutes**
AIMS	**To compare different voices for voice quality, intonation, and speed.**

MATERIALS   A tape recorder.

PREPARATION   Record five or six short excerpts (of roughly 30 seconds each) of different people speaking. Try to include some famous people speaking in English whose voices the students might not be familiar with (for example, the Queen, a famous sporting personality, a singer—they need not be native speakers of English). Make sure that you know a few details about each speaker, such as age and job.

PROCEDURE   1 Draw the scales below on the board and ask the students to draw a separate copy of them for each of the voices they are going to hear (or give them photocopies).

2 Discuss with the students some of the features of a person's voice which might convey something about them. What features of a voice, for example, might give the impression that the speaker was young or old?

interesting _____	boring
kind _____	cruel
intelligent _____	stupid
friendly _____	unfriendly
old _____	young
brave _____	cowardly

Photocopiable © Oxford University Press

3 Play the excerpts and ask the students to put a mark on each scale to show their impressions of each speaker.

4 Ask the students to compare their impressions with another student.

5 Discuss the impressions and how they were conveyed. Then tell the students the identity of the speakers. Were their impressions correct?

3.15 Is this person about to stop speaking?

LEVEL   All

TIME   5–10 minutes

AIMS   **To recognize when people are likely to begin or finish a turn of speaking.**

MATERIALS   A tape recorder.

PREPARATION

1 Record a conversation or interview in which the speakers take frequent turns. It should be an authentic piece of listening material, if possible. It does not matter if it is above the students' present level of English, since they will be listening for acoustic rather than verbal signals for turn-taking.

2 Decide on some points where you will stop the tape. Some of the points should be in the middle of what the person is saying, and some should be at the end of a turn of speaking.

PROCEDURE

1 Play the tape and stop it at the first point you decided on. Ask the students to say whether they think the person has finished speaking or not.

2 Elicit/explain that you can tell when a person is about to stop speaking because they will:
  - slow down
  - speak more clearly
  - often speak on a falling tone.

3 Play the next section of the tape so that the students can check if they were right or not.

4 Repeat for the other points on your tape.

COMMENTS

The ability to tell when someone is finishing speaking is useful in conversations.

3.16 Attitudes

LEVEL

All

TIME

10 minutes

AIMS

To help judge the mood of speakers by using clues such as intonation, facial expression, and gestures.

MATERIALS

A video recorder.

PREPARATION

1 Record 2–3 minutes of a soap opera or a sitcom from English-language television. It should be an excerpt in which the participants go through one or more changes of mood.

2 Design a table like the one on the next page, in which the students mark the moods of the speakers. Fill in the answer to the first utterance.

Utterance number												
	1	2	3	4	5	6	7	8	9	10	11	12
excited												
bored												
friendly	✔											
suspicious												
angry												
amused												
surprised												
pleased												
neutral												
other												

Photocopiable © Oxford University Press

PROCEDURE

1 Elicit from the students what clues they use to guess what mood people are in. They will probably suggest things such as how fast or loudly people speak, their intonation, expression, and gestures. Have they noticed any differences between British or American people and people from their own country in these respects?

2 Play the video, stopping it every now and again, and each time ask the students to decide what the people are talking about. They should mark on their table what they think the main mood of the person is for each turn of speaking.

3 Ask the students to compare and discuss their answers with another student.

4 Discuss any problematic answers and give your own.

4 Adapting published materials

Published materials of any kind have to cater for a very wide range of possible users, which means that they cannot address any individual student or group of students directly. Listening materials are usually in the form of an audio or video tape, which distances the original speakers in time and space, and possibly also culturally, from the eventual receivers of the spoken message in the classroom. Although the writers do try to anticipate the probable interests of the students, it would obviously be impossible for the tapes to have a particular individual or class in mind. The students are often placed in the position of being an 'overhearer' or 'judge' of a listening passage, where they have to react at second-hand to a spoken message which was not addressed to them. All these factors combine to create a psychological distance between the students and what they are listening to.

The activities in this chapter do three things to help the students overcome the problems caused by this distance:

- show the students ways of adapting the recordings and the tasks in the coursebook so that they are more personal, i. e. they address those particular students in that particular class
- give the students the opportunity to become participants rather than overhearers
- allow them to 'answer back' to the speaker on the tape
- help them to explore what dialogues on coursebook tapes and videos can tell us (or not tell us) about the ways in which listeners and speakers interact directly in real life.

I have included a couple of activities for manipulating and adapting tasks for listening tests in this chapter; these are designed to help the students become participants in the testing process, or at least to reveal what is being tested and how. I hope, thus, to remove some of the fear which goes with listening tests.

Overcoming the 'overhearer' effect

4.1 Overhearers

LEVEL	**Upper-intermediate and above**
TIME	**40 minutes**
AIMS	**To show students how they can become participants, rather than just 'overhearers'.**
PROCEDURE	1 Give the students copies of the newspaper article, and ask them to read it and say if they agree with what happened in the end.

STOP KNOCKING THE BOSS CHRIS, HE'S BEHIND YOU
Overheard jibes lead to sacking

SALESMAN Chris Smith was sacked after heaping insults on his firm — unaware that his boss was sitting behind him.

Chris spoke his mind as he and managing director Roger Summers sat back-to-back in a crowded Chinese restaurant.

During his meal with colleagues Chris blasted all the computer firm's executives, ran down its products and boasted of his plans to quit for a better job.

The £30,000-a-year salesman only found out that his the boss had been eavesdropping when he got back from lunch – and was fired on the spot.

Compensation

But yesterday he won £10,396 compensation when an industrial tribunal ruled his dismissal from Southend-based Datasure was unfair.

Mr. Summers told the Central London hearing: "He was being disloyal to the company which I saw as gross misconduct.

"He also said he was being head-hunted. I thought he was trying to blackmail us into giving him a rise" Father of four Chris, in his early 30's, said: "They have devastated my life."

He added that his home at South Woodham Ferrers, Essex, had been repossessed.

The panel decided Chris was not given a proper disciplinary hearing.

(from the *Sun*)

2 Ask the students to get into pairs and tell each other about any situations like this where they remember overhearing something they were not meant to hear. What did they do?

3 Ask the pairs to suggest a situation in which it might be embarrassing to be an overhearer, and a situation where the overhearer might be useful to the people he or she is listening to. Write some of the situations on the board.

4 Choose a dialogue from some published material at the students' level, play it, and do the comprehension tasks that go with it, so that you are sure the students have understood it.

5 Ask the pairs of students to pretend to be someone who overhears the dialogue. Who are they? Is it an embarrassing or a helpful situation?

6 Ask the students what they would say if they revealed their presence to the speakers at the end of the dialogue. What do they think might happen next?

7 Ask the class to share their answers.

4.2 Participants

LEVEL	**Upper-intermediate and above**
TIME	**10 minutes**
AIMS	**To encourage the students to become participants rather than overhearers.**
MATERIALS	Tape recorder.
PREPARATION	Choose a conversation or dialogue from the students' coursebook, or some other published listening material at their level.
PROCEDURE	1 Play the dialogue and do the comprehension tasks that go with it, so that you are sure the students have understood it.

2 Divide the class into groups. The groups should be the number of people taking part in the conversation, plus one more—for instance, if there were two people in the conversation on the tape, divide the class into groups of three. Ask the groups to imagine that there is another person taking part in the conversation. Who is it? What is his/her relationship to the other speakers?

3 Ask the groups to prepare a conversation which includes the extra person.

4 Ask a few groups to perform their dialogue. The others listen and try to guess the identity of the extra person. How much or how little of the dialogue has been changed?

Personalizing the listening material

4.3 How do these pictures fit in?

LEVEL	**Lower-intermediate and above**
TIME	**10–15 minutes**
AIMS	**To make published listening material more personal to the students.**

MATERIALS

Tape recorder. A piece of published listening material at the students' level, and the transcript that goes with it. About 10–15 large magazine pictures showing a mixture of scenes, people, and activities. They should have some possible connection to the listening material, although it can be a very vague one. But students would probably have difficulty in using a picture of a waterfall, for instance, if the listening passage is about a journey in the desert.

PROCEDURE

1 Play the listening passage and do the comprehension tasks that go with it, to make sure that the students have understood what it is about.

2 Stick up the magazine pictures where all the students can see them.

3 Put the students in groups of three or four and explain that the pictures illustrate something in the listening passage they have just heard. It might be something that is mentioned explicitly, or it might be something that is below the surface of what they heard, for example, a place they think one of the speakers would have visited.

4 Show the students the transcript, and play the tape again. The groups must now work out how and where the pictures fit into the listening passage, making sure that they give fully worked-out reasons for their decisions.

5 Finally, ask the groups to share and compare what they did with the pictures.

4.4 Character and voice

LEVEL

All

TIME

15–20 minutes

AIMS

To become aware of elements of a person's voice, such as pitch, speed of speaking, accent, and loudness, which give clues to the type of person they are.

MATERIALS

Video recorder and tape recorder. An excerpt from a foreign film of about two minutes in length, which contains about three or four speakers. If you have a monolingual class, choose a film in their language. It does not matter if it has subtitles or not. Also have ready a selection of varied male and female voices from published EFL listening material.

PROCEDURE

1 Ask the students whether films in English are dubbed into their language. Do they think it is a good idea? Are there some actors who are particularly famous for dubbing? Are they close to the original actor's voice? (If you are lucky enough to have an example of a 'dubbed' voice and the original you could play these to the students.)

2 Briefly explain the situation in the film excerpt the students are going to see. Tell the students that they should watch and make notes about the characters' appearances, ages, and personalities. Play the excerpt.

3 Ask the students to compare their impressions of the characters in pairs.

4 Tell the students that this film is going to be dubbed into English, and that they are responsible for choosing the voices that will do the dubbing.

5 Play the selection of male and female voices (it is a good idea to number them as you play them), and ask the pairs to choose the one they think would be best for each part in the original film.

6 Pool the suggestions and see if the class can reach a consensus.

7 **(Optional)** Ask the students which English-speaking actors they would like to play each part if this film was remade in a Hollywood version, and what it is about their voices that makes them suitable.

FOLLOW-UP

If the students want, in groups they could try dubbing the excerpt they have seen; they will have to translate the dialogue into English first.

4.5 Word bingo

LEVEL	**All**
TIME	**10 minutes**
AIMS	**To listen for particular words in a stream of speech; to re-use familiar listening material with a task which the students have designed.**
MATERIALS	Tape recorder.
PREPARATION	Select a one- to two-minute excerpt from some published listening material which the students are using as part of their course, or have used before in class. Make sure that there is a transcript of it in the teacher's book.
PROCEDURE	1 Tell or remind the students about the topic of the tape they are going to hear.
	2 Ask the students to draw a 'bingo card' with nine squares and to write nine words on it they think they will hear. Tell them that 'a', 'the', and forms of the verbs 'be', 'have', and 'do' are not allowed, but anything else is.
	3 Play the tape. The students cross off words on their cards as they hear them.
	4 The first student to cross off all his/her words is the winner. If no one finishes, then the student with the most words crossed off is the winner. You may want to check whether they are correct against the transcript.
FOLLOW-UP	At the end of the activity you could give the students the transcript so that they can see if they missed hearing any of the words on their card.

4.6 Our questions and answers

LEVEL	**Lower-intermediate and above**
TIME	**20–30 minutes**
AIMS	**To listen for detail; to help the students to make their own listening tasks.**
MATERIALS	Some published listening material at the students' level and a tape recorder.

PROCEDURE	1 Play the listening material and do the comprehension tasks that go with it, so that you are sure the students have understood it.
	2 Divide the students into an equal number of pairs.
	3 Ask the class to listen to the tape again, and then in their pairs to write four questions about the information on the tape. They must also write down the answers.
	4 Ask each pair to get together with another pair. The pairs should take it in turns to read out their questions. If the other pair have an answer which fits the question, they get a point. The winners are the pair with the most points.
	5 **(Optional)** The students could compare the questions they wrote to the ones in the published materials—which, in their opinion, were better and why?
COMMENTS	This is useful practice for listening tests such as FCE because gives the students the experience of being question setters.

4.7 From answer to question 1

LEVEL	**Intermediate and above**
TIME	**10–15 minutes**
AIMS	**To encourage the use of questions to predict what will be said in short extracts.**
MATERIALS	Tape recorder; practice tests for FCE or CAE.
PREPARATION	You will need a practice test for Paper 4 of the Cambridge First Certificate or Advanced English examinations, or published material at any level which asks this type of question, and the tape that goes with it. Find the section which asks the students to listen to a series of short extracts and answer questions on them. A typical FCE question might look like this:

> Listen to this businessman phoning a colleague. Why has he phoned?
>
> A to change his plans
> B to arrange a meeting
> C to apologize

and a CAE question like this:

> For questions 31–35, match the extracts as you hear them with the topics listed A to G.
>
> A painting competition
> B prize-winning roses
> C horse show
> D playing tennis
> E an award-winning design
> F competition in a newspaper
> G general knowledge quiz

Make copies of these questions.

PROCEDURE

1 Ask the students to get into pairs and choose one of the answers. They should prepare the dialogue they think they might hear for that answer.

2 Ask some of the pairs to act out their dialogues. The rest of the class listen, and choose the right answer. They can also discuss what clues they used to choose the answer.

3 Play the tape for the practice test or other published material, and ask the students to answer the questions. They will now find it much easier to do so.

4.8 From answer to question 2

LEVEL

Intermediate and above

TIME

20 minutes

AIMS

To help recognize ideas which are restated in other words; to show that the correct answer in a multiple-choice listening task often rephrases a word or words on the tape.

MATERIALS

Tape recorder.

PREPARATION

1 Find some multiple-choice questions in published material or a practice test, and make copies for the students. If you refer to the tape or the transcript, you will find that many of the correct answers have been said in other words on the tape. For example, the tape might use the word 'distribute', which is paraphrased in answer B in the following question:

> The manager asked her colleague to
>
> A write a report
> B hand out a report
> C send the report to Tom.

2 Listen to the tape and notice which words in the correct answers which have been rephrased on the tape. Underline the words in the correct answers and make copies of the questions and answers.

PROCEDURE

1 Give the students copies of the questions and answers and ask them to rephrase the words you have underlined.
2 Discuss some of the different ways in which the students have rephrased the words.
3 Play the tape while the students check whether they have rephrased the words in the same way as the tape.

COMMENTS

This is useful for FCE, CAE, and CPE exam practice, as well as listening skills in general.

4.9 Filtered listening

LEVEL

Lower-intermediate and above

TIME

10 minutes

AIMS

To help pick out important information in a situation with background noise.

MATERIALS

Two tape recorders.

PREPARATION

1 Find two listening passages of roughly equal length from the coursebook, which the students have already done some time ago. One should be of male voices, the other, female.
2 Write five comprehension questions to go with each passage. Make enough copies of each set of questions for half the class.

PROCEDURE

1 Divide the class into two halves and distribute each set of questions to half the class.
2 Tell the students that they must listen and answer the questions for their listening passage. The problem will be that there will be two passages playing at the same time, and they must try to ignore the other passage and just concentrate on their own.
3 Play the two passages simultaneously while the students try to do their task. You will probably need to play the tapes several times.

4.10 Changing the listening passage

LEVEL

Upper-intermediate and above

TIME

30 minutes

AIMS

To analyse listening difficulties; to adapt listening materials to meet the students' needs.

MATERIALS

A piece of published listening material at the students' level and a tape recorder.

PROCEDURE

1 Play the listening material and do the comprehension tasks that go with it.

2 After the class have completed the tasks, ask them to fill in the questionnaire below.

3 In pairs ask the class to suggest three changes they would make to the listening material to make it more interesting and valuable for language learning.

Your feelings about this listening passage

1 Did you get the overall meaning the first time it was played?
Yes/No

2 Did you find the topic interesting?
Yes/No

Why/Why not? _____

_____

If not, what would have made it more interesting? Tick (✓) one or more of the following:

– change the speakers?
– provide some visuals?
– change the topic?
– give more information about the topic?
– change the tasks?

Any other suggestions?

3 Name some points in the tape where you had difficulty in understanding.

4 Say if these things caused you problems (1 = none, 5 = a lot)

speed	1	2	3	4	5
accents	1	2	3	4	5
understanding the topic	1	2	3	4	5
vocabulary/structures	1	2	3	4	5
tasks	1	2	3	4	5

Any other things? What were they?

Listening to dialogues

4.11 Predict a dialogue

LEVEL   All

TIME   15–20 minutes

AIMS   **To anticipate what a speaker is going to say.**

MATERIALS   A tape recorder; coursebook recording.

PREPARATION
1 Choose six or eight consecutive exchanges from the beginning of a dialogue on the tape which goes with a coursebook. You will usually be able to find the transcript of the dialogue at the end of the students' coursebook or in the Teacher's Book.
2 Write down the exchanges in jumbled order. For example, I used Tapescript 7, 'A disastrous holiday', from *Headway Intermediate*:

A: What happened? Did you fall out, have rows and things?

B: Oh yes, oh quite a few actually.

A: Which was the worst?

A: Oh no!

B: No, no it was not that. The first thing that went wrong was that the country we were going to decided to have a war a few days before we were going there.

B: Mmm. So that was the end of that. But the plane we were going on was stopping at Rome, so rather than not having a holiday at all, we thought we would go to Italy

A: Tell me, have you ever had a holiday that went wrong?

B: The worst? Well, I suppose it was while I was at university my girlfriend Susan and I had two weeks well no, no, one week, one week of absolute hell and then things got a bit better.

---

3 Find the relevant section on the tape.

PROCEDURE
1 Give the students copies of the jumbled dialogue and ask them to get into pairs and see if they can put it in the right order.
2 When they think they have got the right order, play the tape to the end of the section you have given them so that they can check if they were correct. Ask the students what clues they used to help them.

3 Discuss who they think the two speakers are, and the other people mentioned in the dialogue. What is the situation? What do they think is going to happen next? Ask the pairs to invent a continuation of the dialogue. Give them about five minutes to do this.

4 Ask a few pairs act or read out their dialogue.

5 Play the rest of the tape and ask the students to listen and see if any of the topics they had in their dialogue were also mentioned on the tape. Which, in their opinion, was the most interesting dialogue?

4.12 How authentic?

LEVEL

Upper-intermediate and above

TIME

30 minutes

AIMS

To sensitize students to the ways in which speakers and listeners take turns.

MATERIALS

A tape recorder to record the students; a dialogue from published material.

PREPARATION

1 Choose a dialogue from published material that is below the students' present level of English. Have the relevant section of tape ready to play, and make some copies of the transcript.

2 Prepare some role cards which will help the students to produce a similar dialogue to the one on the tape. Here are some I prepared for a dialogue from the *New Cambridge English Course 1*, Lesson 4C:

Student A
Ring your friend and ask how he/she and his/her mother are. Tell the friend that you have got a new boy/girlfriend. Ask about his/her new boy/girlfriend. You gradually discover you have got the same boy/girlfriend.

Student B
Reply to your friend's questions. Tell him/her you have got a new boy/girlfriend too. You gradually discover you have got the same boy/girlfriend.

PROCEDURE

1 Give copies of the role cards to the students and ask them, in pairs, to role-play the dialogue on their cards.

2 Get some of the pairs to act (or read) out their dialogues for the rest of the class and record a couple of the best ones.

3 Play the published dialogue and ask them to compare their versions and the published one. Give them the transcript of the published version so that they can follow it more easily. Play the two best student versions as well. Do they notice any differences? Ask them to listen and notice the following:

  a In their own versions, does one person do more talking than the other? What about the published version—do the two people take roughly equal turns at speaking?

  b Do the speakers use full sentences or do they sometimes reply with short answers like 'Yes', 'so am I', and so on?

  c Does what the speakers say seem psychologically 'right', i. e. the way people would react to each other in real life? For instance, do the people in the different versions of the conversation really listen and react to each other? Do they keep repeating each other's names in a rather strange way?

  d Do their versions have hesitations, like 'um', 'er', and so on? What about the published version? What other differences do they notice?

4 Discuss the differences in the light of the notes below:

  a Often, listening materials in coursebooks have a 'hidden agenda' to practise structures or vocabulary as well as listening skills.

  b In coursebook conversations, people are often more explicit and spell out things more than they would tend to in real life because they are talking for the benefit of 'overhearers' who do not know the situation.

  c Often in real-life casual conversations, one person will have quite a long 'turn' on a subject they are interested in, while the other person listens. It is rare that you get a long series of short exchanges in a real conversation— although you might if it is a more businesslike 'transaction' between people who do not know each other very well.

  d Sometimes, people in coursebook dialogues fail to react properly to what they are being told. That is probably because both parts in the dialogue are written by the same author, so it is sometimes difficult to write it from two people's points of view.

5 Finally, ask the students which version they prefer as a language learner. They will often choose the coursebook version as being clearer and easier to imitate.

VARIATION

If you have access to native speakers, give them a copy of the role cards and record them doing the dialogue. The students will be interested in comparing them with the published material.

4.13 Monologue to dialogue

LEVEL	**Lower-intermediate and above**
TIME	**20–25 minutes**
AIMS	**To recognize how speakers signal the end of a turn of speaking.**
MATERIALS	A tape recorder with a tape-to-tape copying facility; recording of a dialogue.

PREPARATION

1 Choose a dialogue from published listening materials which is slightly below the current level of English of your students.

2 Record only one of the participants in the dialogue and omit the other speaker, as follows:
   - insert your master cassette and a blank cassette into your tape recorder
   - press the record button and record up to the sections you want to omit
   - press your pause button on for the section you want to leave out and turn it off again when the section has passed.

   Do this for each time that the second person in the dialogue speaks.

3 Write or type a continuous transcript of what the first speaker says, without any spaces which might indicate where the second speaker comes in. Make copies for the students. Here is an example from *New Cambridge English Course 3*, Lesson E2:

> Hello, Mary. What's the matter? No, he hasn't. He's just rung me. He's staying with an old friend; he asked me to tell you. He couldn't get through. No, actually, I don't think he did. But Mary. He said …

PROCEDURE

1 Give the students a brief idea of the situation and the roles of the speakers, for example, a wife phoning her husband's friend because she is worried about him.

2 Give the students a copy of the transcript and ask them to mark where they think the second speaker said something. Ask them what kind of clues they used to decide.

3 Now play the tape and ask the students if they want to change any of their decisions. What clues on the tape made them want to make changes, if any?

4 Ask the students, in pairs, to decide what the missing speaker said.

5 Play the original tape so that students can compare it with their own version.

6 Ask the students which they think is the best version, theirs or the one on the tape, and why.

VARIATION

For lower-level students you can make Step 2 easier by telling them the number of times the other person spoke.

5 Using authentic listening material

The aim of this chapter is to provide the students with some strategies for coping with real-life listening of the kind which puts the listener in the role of 'audience' (radio and television programmes, lectures, audio books, and so on). When listening to these types of text, it is often difficult or impossible for the listener to stop speakers and ask them to repeat or clarify something he or she has missed or failed to understand. The speakers usually assume, too, that their audience are native users of the language, and so they make no concessions for non-native speakers in terms of things like speed or accent. Yet this kind of listening is very motivating for language learners, because it gives them information about current world events and the target culture, and puts them in touch with the world outside the confines of the classroom and the school.

One of the aims of the activities in this chapter is to try to make this kind of listening easier for learners by helping them to see that, because of their subject matter and the particular audience they are aimed at, these types of text are often organized in certain predictable ways. The activities also show ways of listening at different levels to the same kind of text, so that students of different abilities can be successful in understanding something useful from these real-life listening materials.

Listening to the news

5.1 News for all

LEVEL	All
TIME	10–20 minutes
AIMS	**To enable all students, whatever their level, to understand something in a news broadcast; to build up listening comprehension skills over a period.**
MATERIALS	A tape recorder.

PREPARATION

Record a short excerpt from television or radio news in English (about five minutes, no longer) in which brief headlines of the main news stories are given before longer versions of the same stories.

PROCEDURE

1 For students of all levels, start by asking them to predict what they think will be in the news that day.

2 Then do one of the following activities, depending on the level of the students.

Beginners to elementary

Play just the headlines (about one minute). Ask them how many news stories there are. Ask them to notice how the newsreader's tone falls at the end of one news item, and starts the next on a higher tone. Play the excerpt again and ask them to note down any words they recognize. Pool the words and ask the students what they think the news stories will be (this can be in the students' native language).

Elementary

Make a list of proper names which appear in the news for the students to tick as they hear them (the first time the list can be in the order the words appear in the broadcast, the second time the words can be in jumbled order).

or

Ask the students to listen and write down any numbers they hear.

or

Ask the students to do a matching exercise in which they draw an arrow to link the name of a place or person in a news story to a word in the same news story, for example:

Tony Blair	new record
Clinton	budget
Ireland	visit
Beatles	divorce law

Lower-intermediate

Play just the headlines (about one minute). Ask the students to note down the three Ws—who, where, and what—for each news item. Ask the students which piece of news they would like to hear in more detail. Ask them to predict what further details they will hear. Play the relevant news story in sections, asking the students to note down any important points they understand. Get the students to pool their notes, and play the news item again, so that they can check their answers.

Intermediate

As for lower-intermediate, then get them to transcribe a couple of sentences from the news story and mark the stressed words.

Upper-intermediate

As for intermediate, but before they listen to the longer version of one of the news stories, ask them to decide on some roles and then listen in one of the roles (see 2.8). After listening, they should compare their notes with people who took different roles.

Advanced
As for intermediate, but after listening and note-taking for the longer version of the story, give the students a newspaper article which is about the same news story. Ask them to prepare an update on the news story which incorporates the information they have heard and read, and which takes the story further. Ask the students to record or read out some of their news stories if there is time.

COMMENTS

It is a good idea to do this activity on a regular basis over a period of time, moving from simpler to more challenging tasks as the students' listening skills improve.

Audiences for the news

5.2 News values

LEVEL

Upper-intermediate and above

TIME

40–50 minutes

AIMS

To help the students to anticipate what they will hear; to listen for gist.

MATERIALS

A tape recorder; the information sheet opposite.

PREPARATION

Before the lesson, record the news headlines from radio or television (usually one or two minutes at the beginning of a five-minute news summary given on the hour) at two separate times a couple of hours apart.

PROCEDURE

1 Before you play the news broadcasts, ask the students to suggest some stories they would expect to hear in the news that day. Write all the suggestions on the board.

2 Explain to the students that radio and television stations have a lot of news stories to choose from, and they tend to broadcast the items which contain the greatest number of 'news values'. Distribute the information sheet opposite and ask the students to read it and in pairs to decide which news values each story on the board contains—they will probably find that some stories contain several 'values'. For example, an earthquake in Finland might combine negativity, freshness, and unexpectedness!

NEWS VALUES

negativity—bad news is rated higher than good news.

freshness—the best news is something which has only just happened, rather than something that happened three days ago.

proximity—the news item is more highly rated if it happened nearby, in the same town or country as the audience, rather than a thousand miles away.

unexpectedness—something which is unexpected, rare, or untypical of how we expect a person or a group to behave is more highly rated.

éliteness—the audience likes news which has happened to famous people.

superlativeness—the audience likes news about the highest building, the most violent crime, the oldest living person, and so on.

relevance—the audience will be more interested in a story which affects them personally.

competition—the radio or television station will obviously rate a 'scoop' story very highly, i.e. one that no other station has got yet.

(adapted from *The Language of News Media* by A. Bell)

3 Discuss with the students who the audience for the broadcast you have recorded are likely to be. This will depend on factors such as the type of station and the time of day the news programme was broadcast.

4 Ask the students, still in their pairs, to decide on a 'running order' for the news items on the board, based on the information they have collected on news values. They will need to decide whether some news values are more important than others. For instance, do 'scoops' automatically come first, or should items combining a number of news values come first?

5 Compare and discuss the running order suggested by different pairs.

6 The students now listen to the first news broadcast and note down the 'three Ws'—*who* is involved, *what* happened, *where* it happened—for each news item. They may need to listen more than once. The aim is not to get all the details of each news item, but just the bare outline.

7 Ask the students to discuss the differences between their selection and ordering of the news items and those chosen by the radio or television station. What do they think are the reasons for any differences? Do they think their version of the news or the station's was the better one?

8 Play the second news broadcast, which was recorded some hours after the first one. Ask the students to make notes again of *who*, *what*, and *where* for each news item.

9 The students can then discuss why they think the selection and ordering of news items has changed since the first broadcast. They will find it useful to refer to their list of news values in the discussion.

10 Finally, the students might like to discuss why these particular news values are reflected in the news, and whether they should be.

COMMENTS

The students could follow this activity with 5.3, 'Comparing the news', or by designing their own news broadcast (see 7.4 and 7.6).

5.3 Comparing the news

LEVEL

Intermediate and above

TIME

15–20 minutes

AIMS

To show the students that spoken messages are shaped by the audience they are designed for.

MATERIALS

A tape recorder; the 'News values' sheet from 5.1.

PREPARATION

1 Record the news headlines (just the first minute or so of the news broadcast) on the same day for two radio stations which are aimed at different audiences. For instance, one of the stations could be 'conservative' or 'middle of the road' (in the UK, Radio 3 or 4, or Classic FM might be good examples) and the other station one aimed at to young people (for example, in the UK, Radio 1, or one of the commercial stations in your area). If it is difficult to find two English-language radio stations in your area, you could make use of satellite television stations broadcasting in English which contrast in style, for example, Sky or BBC Worldwide (British) and Worldnet, NBC, or CNN (American).

2 Make copies of the 'News values' sheet from Activity 5.1.

PROCEDURE

1 Discuss what kinds of audiences the two stations tend to attract.

2 Play one station's news headlines, and ask the students to note down a brief idea of what each news story is about.

3 Do the same with the other radio station's headlines.

4 Ask the students to compare the selection and running order of news items for the two stations, using their 'News values' sheet.

Can they explain any differences in terms of the need to appeal to a particular audience?

5 You could also ask more advanced classes whether they have noticed any differences in delivery, for example, the speed at which the newscasters spoke, or their accents, or whether they tended to speak in short, dramatic sentences or with a more level intonation.

VARIATIONS

The students might also like to:
- compare the news headlines for radio and television
- compare the news headlines for a national radio or television station and an international one, for example, the BBC World Service or Voice of America
- compare the news headlines in a newspaper with those on a radio or television station.

Adapting the news

5.4 Shortening the news

LEVEL

Upper-intermediate and above

TIME

20–30 minutes

AIMS

To understand news broadcasts; to listen for main points; to summarize information heard.

MATERIALS

A tape recorder.

PREPARATION

1 Record a short version of the news (about 5 minutes, no longer) in which brief headlines of the main news stories are given before longer versions of the same stories. BBC Radio 4, the BBC World Service, and Voice of America all broadcast this kind of news on the hour.

2 Transcribe just the headlines.

PROCEDURE

1 Play the longer version of one of the news stories (not the headlines) and ask the students to listen and get a general idea of who, where, and what the story is about. At this point they do not need to listen for detail.

2 Check that the students have understood the gist of the story. Ask them if they know anything about this story and what they think about it.

3 Play the section of the tape again and ask the students to note down the main points of the story.

4 Ask the students to get into pairs and pool the information they have noted down.

5 Tell the students that they are news editors and that they have been asked to prepare a dramatic headline for this piece of news—normally one sentence. The students should decide which part of the story the headline should focus on and write it.

6 Ask a few pairs to read out what they have written.

7 Play the original headline, and ask the students to write it down. You will probably need to play it twice. Check what the students have written against your transcript. Which pair came closest to the original headline? Which was the best?

8 Repeat with some of the other news stories.

5.5 The World Service

LEVEL	**Intermediate and above**
TIME	**40–50 minutes**
AIMS	**To show how speakers adapt what they say and their delivery (speed, articulation, and so on) to their listeners; to listen carefully to connected speech and make a transcript.**
MATERIALS	A tape recorder.
PREPARATION	Record one minute of a news broadcast in English.
PROCEDURE	1 Play the broadcast and ask the students to get a general idea of what news items were mentioned. Discuss the students' answers.

2 Play the recording again and ask the students whether they get the impression that this news broadcast was for native speakers or for a wider audience, for example, the BBC World Service, or Voice of America. Do they ever listen to any of these stations? How do they think the language and delivery of the newscasters is adjusted if they are broadcasting in areas where reception might be poor, or the audience might not know a lot of English, or be using the broadcast to learn English? The students may come up with some of the following ideas:

– the newscasters might speak more slowly
– they might put in more pauses
– they might pronounce the words more carefully
– they might use shorter, simpler sentences
– they might try to avoid words with lots of 's' sounds, which can 'hiss' where reception is poor

    – they might repeat words and ideas more

    – they might give more explanation for things which are specific to British or American culture, for example, 'Thanksgiving holiday' instead of just 'Thanksgiving'.

    The students may have other suggestions as well.

3 Ask the class to listen again to the news excerpt which you recorded. This time, they should write down word for word what the newscaster said. Play the excerpt a few words at a time, and then replay the whole thing so that the students can check what they wrote. Get them to compare their transcription with another student to see if they wrote the same thing, and discuss any problems they had in recognizing sounds and words.

4 In pairs, the students should decide on some changes they would make in delivery and language to improve the broadcast for international transmission.

5 A few of the pairs could perform their revision of the news and explain the changes they have made.

5.6 The news expanded

LEVEL	**Upper-intermediate and above**
TIME	**50 minutes**
AIMS	**To integrate listening with the other three skills.**
MATERIALS	A tape recorder.
PREPARATION	Record the news headlines from an English-speaking station, and buy copies of English-language newspapers (enough for one between four students). If you are working in a non-English speaking country, allow for the fact that newspapers in English may arrive a day after the news items are broadcast.
PROCEDURE	1 Play the news headlines and ask the students to make a note of who, where, and what happened for each story.
	2 Play the headlines again and ask the students to note down any other details they heard or were interested in.
	3 Tell the students that they are going to be teams of reporters and news editors.
	4 Ask the groups to choose one of the news stories they are particularly interested in and to pool their notes for that story. They must then decide how they would like to extend the news headline: for example, by sending their reporter somewhere to find out more information, or by interviewing somebody.

5 The group should then refer to their newspaper to see if they can get any more details which might help them. Circulate and help them where necessary.

6 The groups should then either prepare the questions and answers for a short interview, or a report from their roving correspondent.

7 Finally, the students should perform their 'extension of the news' for the rest of the class. If they like, they could record it on a tape recorder or video it.

Other radio or television programmes

5.7 Station surfing

LEVEL	**All**
TIME	**5–10 minutes**
AIMS	**To identify different types of listening texts quickly, using clues such as key words and voice quality.**
MATERIALS	A tape recorder.
PREPARATION	Record a very short extract (about 10–20 seconds) of 8–10 different types of radio programme, for example, music, the news, a phone-in, a play, and so on. The tape will sound as if you are turning the tuner on your radio trying to find a particular radio station.
PROCEDURE	1 Play the tape and ask the students to note down what each programme seems to be about.
	2 Pool the answers. Ask the students how they reached their decisions—they probably relied on making deductions based on words they recognized and on clues to do with features of the voices they heard (such as speed), and whether the speakers sounded calm, angry, or excited. Point out that these are good clues to use.
	3 Ask the students to listen again and check if they were right.
	4 As a final step, you could play the tape again and ask the students to decide what kind of audience each programme would appeal to.
COMMENTS	This activity is also good practice for some of the questions in the Cambridge First Certificate listening exam.

5.8 Weather diary

LEVEL **Intermediate and above**

TIME **30 minutes, then 5–10 minutes a day over a week**

AIMS **To listen for specific information.**

MATERIALS A tape recorder; copies of a weather diary like the one on the next page.

PREPARATION Record the weather forecast for your area each day for a week (in non-English speaking countries, satellite television channels such as Sky or CNN will often give the weather forecast in English for your area).

PROCEDURE
1 Tell the students that they are going to keep a weather diary for a week to see how accurate the professional weather forecasters are!

2 Give the students a list of weather words, and ask them in pairs to sort them into two columns, 'weather we like' and 'weather we don't like'. The list below was drawn up to describe weather in Scotland, and you will need to adapt it to your local weather conditions! The students may find that they disagree about which column to put some of the words in and might need to create another column, 'weather we couldn't agree on'.

wet	dull	cloudy	sunny	foggy
showers	rain	misty	windy	thunderstorms
lightning	gales	snow	frost	ice
sleet	hail	dry	drought	clear

3 Draw the students' attention to some of the key phrases often found in weather forecasts and elicit/explain what they mean. For example:

high/low pressure   fresh   at first/later
brightening up/worsening/clearing   Celsius/Fahrenheit
frequent/heavy/scattered (e.g. showers)
spells/intervals

4 Play the recording you have made for the weather forecast for that day and ask them to note down some key words for:
  – what the weather is going to be like in the area for the next few hours
  – what the weather will be like in 12 hours' time
  – what the weather will be like in 24 hours' time.

(You will find that many forecasts are organized in this way).

5   Show the students an example of a weather diary like the one below. Ask them to draw a chart and note down over the next 24 hours what the weather was really like, and to award the forecaster a big tick (✓) or cross (✗) according to whether he or she got the forecast right or not. (Note: Michael Fish is the name of a BBC weather forecaster.)

THE FISH FORECAST: DID HE GET IT RIGHT?

Richard, Gabriel and Jenny kept a weather diary for five days in May, then compared it to the BBC weather forecast. Check out their results to discover whether Fish and his forecaster friends got it right.

THURSDAY	**FRIDAY**	**SATURDAY**	**SUNDAY**	**MONDAY**
TV forecast Wet, dull, cloudy and misty **Weather** "A bit misty in the morning and it did rain a little in the afternoon. Cloudy too." ✓	**TV forecast** Cloudy in the morning, sunny in the afternoon. Fair chance of rain **Weather** "It rained quite a bit and it was cloudy but is was sunnier in the morning." ✓	**TV forecast** Cloudy outlook with some sun **Weather** "A bit sunny in the morning but then it rained really hard!" ✗	**TV forecast** Rain at first, brightening up later in the day **Weather** "Patchy, hard rain." ✗	**TV forecast** Light showers, brightening up later in the day **Weather** "It didn't rain at all and was quite sunny, but there were some clouds too." ✗

(from the *Daily Telegraph*)

6   Over the next week, play the weather forecast for that day in class and ask the students to keep their diary. Then ask for feedback about the accuracy of the previous day's forecast. If there are different forecasters, are some more accurate than others?

5.9 Sports temperatures

LEVEL   **Lower-intermediate and above**

TIME   **30–40 minutes**

AIMS   **To understand gist.**

MATERIALS   A tape recorder.

PREPARATION
1   Find out what kinds of sports the class enjoy, perhaps by doing a survey of favourite sports in a previous lesson.
2   Record two or three minutes of a sports match between two teams or two or more players for a sport which will be familiar to the students. If possible, it should be a fast sport, such as soccer, American football, tennis, swimming, rugby, or horse-racing, rather than a 'slow' sport like cricket or snooker. It will help if you know the final result of the game—you can usually find out the result from a newspaper. Make sure that you know the names of the players/participants—a newspaper report of the game or race will also be useful for this.

PROCEDURE

1 Play about 30 seconds of the tape and ask the students to identify the sport, and if possible, who is playing/taking part in it.

2 Elicit from the students how much they know about the game, its rules, the equipment you need to play it, and where it usually takes place.

3 Ask the students to draw a 'temperature chart' like the one below, or give them photocopies.

Sports temperature chart

	20 secs	40 secs	60 secs	80 secs	100 secs	140 secs	160 secs	180 secs	200 secs
Excited									
Mood									
Calm									

Photocopiable © Oxford University Press

4 Tell them that they are going to listen to more of the sports broadcast. This time they must mark in what they think is the mood of the commentator for every 20 seconds of the report. The commentator's mood could range from very calm (not much happening), to very excited, with a lot happening. By the end of the broadcast they will have produced something which looks like a patient's temperature chart in hospital, except in their case it will show the commentator's changes in mood. Discuss how they will recognize these changes in mood—for example, the commentator might talk faster or slower, louder or more quietly, with many or a few changes in intonation, and so on. Show them the sample chart on the next page to give them an idea of what they are aiming to do.

5 The students should listen to the whole recorded excerpt and fill in the chart. It might be helpful to tell them when each 20 seconds is up.

6 The students should compare their chart with a neighbour's. Was it an exciting excerpt from the game or was it rather uneventful? If it was a recent game they know about or watched, is this excerpt typical of the overall mood of the game?

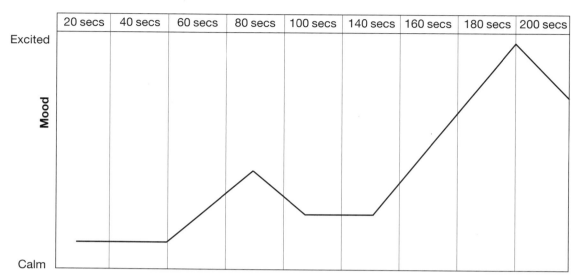

	20 secs	40 secs	60 secs	80 secs	100 secs	140 secs	160 secs	180 secs	200 secs

Excited

Mood

Calm

FOLLOW-UP

1 Ask the students to draw up a chart like the one below in which there is a column for each team, or in the case of an individual sport like tennis, swimming, or horse-racing, a column for each participant. For team games like football, you might like to get the students to help you write up the members of each team on the board—the sports enthusiasts in the class will be happy to help you, but it is probably a good idea to do it fairly briskly, in case the rest of the class get bored!

Participants chart

Manchester United	Wolves
✓✓✓	✓✓✓✓

2 Play the excerpt again. Ask the students to listen and to tick the appropriate column each time they hear that team or player mentioned. You will probably need to play the excerpt a couple of times.

3 The students can then compare their answers and see if there is any connection between the number of times each player or team was mentioned and the final result of the game. Did the team, player, or horse which was mentioned the most win in the end, or not?

5.10 Listening to politicians

LEVEL Advanced

TIME 30 minutes

AIMS To listen critically; to attend to the main message and filter out irrelevancies.

MATERIALS A tape recorder.

PREPARATION

1 Tape 2–3 minutes of a politician being interviewed or a discussion between politicians. Many English-speaking countries now both film and record for radio the daily proceedings in Parliament or Congress, and this would provide ideal material. Another good source of material is morning news programmes in which politicians are interviewed (such as the *Today* programme on BBC Radio 4). If you want to steer clear of discussing the politics of the country you are teaching in, you could record politicians from an English-speaking country via satellite or the World Service.

2 If you have time, make a transcript of what the politicians say or get the students to make their own transcript after Step 2 below.

PROCEDURE

1 Play the recording once and ask the students to name the topic under discussion. Ask them if they can identify the politician(s), or catch their names, and if they know which political party (or parties) they represent.

2 Discuss the students' answers.

3 Play the recording a second time, this time allowing the students to refer to the transcript while they listen.

4 Ask the students to get into pairs and underline the main message of what the politician(s) are saying, and to indicate with brackets any words, phrases, or sentences which they think are irrelevant to that message.

5 Discuss with the students what kinds of items they have put in brackets. They will probably find they have included words, phrases, and sentences which:
   – go into past history, not the present situation
   – talk about a related subject, not the one they were asked about
   – attack the other political party/parties
   – defend their own party
   – use special political jargon which nobody else understands.

It is interesting to see how much of what the politician has said is left after all the irrelevant bits have been edited out!

VARIATION 1

If you and the students do not have time to make a transcript, at Step 3 the students can just listen several times and note down ten words, phrases, or sentences which they think the politician(s) could well omit because they are not necessary. The students will find it more difficult to do without the transcript.

VARIATION 2

Instead of editing for irrelevance, you could tell the students that they have to edit for time, and somehow lose 30 seconds of the broadcast because the programme is over–running. They must get rid of the 30 seconds without distorting the politicians' message. Alternatively, they could pretend that they only have 30 seconds and must select the best 'sound bite' from the whole excerpt.

VARIATION 3

As an alternative to irrelevance, the students could edit for insincerity.

5.11 Radio advertisements

LEVEL

Beginner and elementary

TIME

30 minutes

AIMS

To listen for particular information.

MATERIALS

A tape recorder.

PREPARATION

1 Record four to five advertisements from English-speaking commercial radio stations. (Television advertisements are not really suitable, because most of the message tends to be conveyed through the visuals used, rather than the words.)
2 Prepare a jumbled list of words on the tape which are used to describe the products—see Step 2 below.

PROCEDURE

1 Play the advertisements and ask the students to identify the products or services which are being advertised. Write them on the board.
2 Give the students a jumbled list of words used on the tape to describe the products. Ask them to listen again and identify which words go with which product.
3 Divide the students into pairs. Ask each pair to choose a product and think of four words or phrases which could be used to describe it. They can use some of the words from the tape, or words that they already know. They could also use a dictionary, and learn some new words. For butter, for example, they might produce *yellow*, *delicious*, *square*, and *with bread*. Circulate and help the pairs, and at the same time collect the names of the products they have chosen.

4 Write the names of the products on the board.

5 Play the tape again, and ask the students to listen particularly to the intonation used. Does it fall and rise on particular types of words? (The main stress and highest pitch will probably be on the qualities and names the advertisers wish to stress.)

6 Ask each pair to 'perform' their advertisement, using the words from Step 3 and copying the intonation of the original. The rest of the class have to listen and decide which of the products on the board is being described. If they wish, they can vote for the best advertisement.

VARIATION

For intermediate-level students and above

1 Ask the students to listen to the tape again and decide individually which they think is the best advertisement.

2 Put the students in pairs and ask them to explain to each other why they chose that particular advertisement. Suggest that they use these criteria to justify their choice:

music   voice   repetition
connotations   originality

FOLLOW-UP

Ask the students, in groups of three or four, to design and record their own radio advertisement, for example, for an event they want to publicize, or for a product they saw advertised on television, a charity, or to attract visitors to their town. You could also take in some examples of magazine or newspaper advertisements for the students to convert into radio advertisements. One or two members of the group could do the 'voice-over', and the others compose and sing the background 'jingle' to go with it.

5.12 Opinion programmes

LEVEL

Advanced

TIME

10–15 minutes

AIMS

To listen for the language of opinion

MATERIALS

A tape recorder.

PREPARATION

Record about five minutes of a radio or television opinion programme—in Britain *Any Questions* or *Any Answers* (which now includes a phone-in section) would be ideal; the BBC World Service also broadcasts opinion programmes such as *International Question Time* and *In the Lion's Den*.

PROCEDURE

1 Tell the students the first question they will hear and ask them how much they know about the background to this question. Ask them to decide how they would answer the question and then ask some of the students to give their opinion as if they were answering on the programme.

2 Play the question and one of the replies that the students can compare their answer with the one given on the programme.

3 Elicit from the students some of the phrases they might use for expressing opinions, for example:
Well, I think …
As far as I'm concerned …
If it were up to me …
I do not really know if …

4 Ask the students to listen again and check if any of the phrases were used.

5 Repeat Steps 1 to 4 with another question and answer.

Other kinds of authentic material

5.13 Lectures

LEVEL

Intermediate and above

TIME

30 minutes

AIMS

To listen for information; to take notes effectively.

MATERIALS

A tape recorder.

PREPARATION

1 Either find a published recording of an excerpt from a lecture, for example, *Study Listening* by Tony Lynch or, if you are working in an academic setting, ask a lecturer if they would be willing to record themselves talking about a subject for 10 minutes, or even to come and give a short lecture to your students. Ask them if they can give you a copy of their lecture notes in advance, or tell you the main points of what they are going to say.

2 Make your own notes, only including the important points, and using abbreviations and symbols. Add about ten false facts which have nothing to do with the subject of the lecture, or which could not be true. Make copies of your notes.

PROCEDURE

1 Tell the students the title of the lecture and ask them to predict some of the information they might hear. Write their suggestions on the board.

2 Give copies of your notes to the students and give them a few minutes to read them and see if any of the predicted information appears in them.

3 Tell the students that you have included ten items of information which they will not hear in the lecture, and that they must cross these out as they listen. Play the tape or listen to the lecture.

4 Discuss the answers.

5 Ask the students to make their own notes, remembering as much as they can from the lecture, without referring to your notes. If you have the lecture on tape, you could play it again.

COMMENTS

Note-taking is difficult for students. One way of guiding them into better note-taking is to get them to analyse good examples of notes (the teacher's notes in this activity) or to compare their notes with another student's (as in 1.8).

5.14 Audio books 2

LEVEL

Upper-intermediate and above

TIME

20 minutes

AIMS

To introduce the students to 'audio books' and to encourage them to listen to these outside class.

MATERIALS

Two pages from a novel and an audio recording of it. The audio version should be an abridged, i.e. a shortened, version of the novel. If the students are doing a set book for an examination you could use the full-length version of the novel they are studying. A tape recorder.

PREPARATION

1 Copy the two pages of the book.

2 Prepare some reading comprehension tasks for the first page.

PROCEDURE

1 Give the students copies of the first page from the book. Treat it as you would a reading comprehension text. Do the comprehension tasks so that you are sure that the students have understood the text.

2 Play the part of the tape that corresponds to the first page and ask the students what differences they noticed between the two versions and why they think these changes were made when the book was recorded on tape.

3 Give out the copies of the second page. Treat it like a reading comprehension text as in Step 1.

4 Ask the students, in pairs, to decide what they would leave out if they were going to adapt this page for reading on to a cassette. Discuss the suggestions. What do they reveal about the differences between reading a story and listening to it?

5 Play the part of the cassette that corresponds to the second page. Ask the students to note down the differences between the spoken and written versions.

6 Finally, ask the students to compare their suggestions for adaptation with the changes that were actually made in the taped version.

6 Telephoning

Telephoning in a foreign language tends to be an extremely stressful activity. There are a number of reasons for this. You are often telephoning strangers (if you were phoning family and friends you might use your own language). When you are telephoning, you cannot see the person you are speaking to, or their expressions, gestures, or surroundings, and so you miss a lot of the clues which usually help you to understand the meaning of what they are saying. It seems to be more difficult to ask people to repeat things on the telephone than it would be if you were speaking to them face-to-face. There is also the problem of unfamiliar 'telephone language', such as *just connecting you*, or the formulas which staff in businesses are now taught to use when answering the telephone, such as *Hello, this is Edinburgh Insurance, Diane speaking; how may I help you?*, all said extremely fast. Digitized messages, such as *You are through to the Gaiety Cinema. If you require the times of programmes, press 1. If you want to book a ticket, press 2* are also common now. Finally, telephone habits vary from culture to culture. Some cultures, for instance, put most or all of the responsibility on the caller for identifying him/herself and pursuing what he or she wants, and some make the recipient equally responsible for doing so.

I have found it best to lead the students gently through several stages before they actually make telephone calls to people they do not know:

Stage 1
Help the students to find their way around telephone directories. This is a non-threatening way of introducing them to reasons for making telephone calls and to ways of finding out telephone numbers. It is a good idea to start with the 'white pages' and 'yellow pages' of telephone directories—to show them the ways in which these are organized and the kind of information they contain. If you are in a non-English speaking country, there is nothing to stop you using the local directories, because this will also give you and the students the chance to identify possible English-speaking individuals and companies in your town who can be used when the students actually reach the stage of making telephone calls (see Activities 6.3 and 6.4).

Stage 2

Teach 'telephone language' and how to be polite on the telephone, for example:

> *Hello, I wonder if I could speak to …*
> *Thanks for your help.*
> *Would it be possible to leave a message for her/him?*

At this stage the students could also practise role-playing telephone calls to each other in class (see Activity 6.1).

Stage 3

Get the students to make real telephone calls, but to each other, so that they are speaking to familiar and tolerant listeners (see Activities 6.3 and 6.4).

Stage 4

Finally, the students should be confident enough to make transactional telephone calls to strangers, although you might still want to rehearse the conversations first in class. You could also help students towards this final stage by recording typical answering messages from companies and information lines (you can buy a simple telephone attachment which will enable you to do this) and playing them in class with an accompanying task, so that the students get used to this kind of telephoning (see Activity 6.6).

6.1 Your telephone personality

LEVEL	**Upper-intermediate and above**
TIME	**20 minutes**
AIMS	**To encourage the students to analyse how well they listen to other people on the telephone.**
MATERIALS	A tape recorder; copies of pages 110–11.
PREPARATION	1 Find a recording of a telephone conversation at the students' level—there will probably be one in their coursebook—or record one of your own telephone conversations by leaving the answering machine running when you answer the telephone.
	2 Make some role cards so that the students can also act out the conversation. For example, I made these role cards for the telephone conversation in *Headway Intermediate*, Unit 8, tapescript 21:

> **Landlord/landlady**
> You have a room for rent. Angela rings you up to enquire about it. Give Angela the information she wants about the room. Give her directions about how to get to you.

> **Angela**
> You have seen an advertisement for a room for rent. Ring up the landlord/landlady and ask for information about the room: price, what the rent includes, house rules, and public transport. Ask if you can come and see the place.

Make copies of 'Your phone personality' (see pages 110–11).

PROCEDURE

1 Divide the students into pairs, give them the role cards, and ask them to act out the telephone call.

2 Draw the four shapes below on the board and ask the students to choose quickly, without thinking about it too much, the symbol which they think best reflects their personality. They should then pick another, second symbol.

3 Give the students the handout on the four 'phone personalities'. Ask them to read it and say whether they think the analysis of their personality, based on the shapes they chose, is true. Did they show any of that behaviour in the role play they have just done?

4 Play the recording of the telephone conversation. Ask the students whether the speakers seem to belong to any of the four 'phone personalities'.

5 Ask the students to write down one good point and one bad point about their own phone personality. Pool some of the things the students have written. Suggest that they might try analysing the phone personality of the person on the other end of the telephone the next time they make or receive a telephone call!

YOUR PHONE PERSONALITY

Your choice of symbols can reveal a lot about your personality and the way you use the phone.

The first symbol you chose reveals the most dominant aspect of your personality. The second symbol tells you about a less powerful, but still very influential part of your character.

The aspirer

You've chosen the only symbol with a clear sense of direction. You have a clear sense of where you are going and the goals you are trying to reach. You are brisk and businesslike on the phone, and you get to the point quickly. You tend to finish the call quickly after you've achieved your purpose. You have a lot of phones all over the place and you're a big user of mobile phones. You like phones because they allow you to communicate quickly and accurately. You use the language of achievement a lot, for example, 'planning ahead', 'making progress'.

The admirer

You've chosen the most harmonious symbol. You are a warm and sympathetic person who really understands and listens to other people. You can often read between the words and are sensitive to the unsaid things in telephone conversations. You don't like telephones all that much; you'd rather meet the person face-to-face. But you can actually be very persuasive on the phone. You tend to let the other person do a lot of the talking and they can get a bit worried by the silence on the other end of the phone! You tend to use language like 'My feeling is', 'My intuition is'.

§

The inspirer

You've chosen the symbol with the most energy. You have lots of energy and ideas and you like being involved in a number of activities at the same time. You'll probably doodle while you phone, and you like phones with loudspeakers so that you're free to move about while you're making your phone call. You radiate enthusiasm and you tend to say things like 'That sounds wonderful', 'I've got a great idea'. You talk quite quickly, and are good at suggesting solutions to problems, but you're not the most patient telephoner in the world.

The enquirer

You've chosen the most logical symbol. You are a logical, methodical, and careful thinker. You like the telephone because you can quickly check up on information, and you like the facilities that enable you to store numbers on your telephone, find out how many people have been calling you, and so on. You think answering machines are a great invention. You may be a little slow in replying to what someone says to you on the phone, but that's because you want to be sure you're saying the right thing when you reply. When you do reply, you speak slowly and carefully, reflecting on your words. You use language like 'Let's think this through' or 'The way I see it'.

(Adapted from *Be Your Own Boss*)

6.2 Mobile telephone

LEVEL	**Elementary and above**
TIME	**10 minutes**
AIMS	**To predict the other side of a telephone conversation.**
MATERIALS	A mobile telephone.

PREPARATION

Either arrange for someone to ring you at a pre-arranged time during the class, and plan what you are going to say, or plan an imaginary conversation you are going to have with someone over the telephone.

PROCEDURE

1 Start the class as normal. The telephone will ring suddenly (if you are doing the imaginary telephone call, secretly adjust your telephone so that it rings).

2 Look very surprised, and ask the class if they would mind if you answered it. Have a brief conversation (6–10 exchanges), adjusting your language to the level of the class. Human curiosity being what it is, you will be guaranteed to have the full attention of the class.

3 Finish the telephone call, and then ask the class to discuss in pairs:
   - who was calling you
   - what the topic was
   - where the person was calling from.

   For intermediate-level and above, you could also add:
   - what the mood was
   - what will be the next thing to happen as a result of the conversation.

4 Pool the answers.

Acknowledgements
Verri Toste invented this activity.

6.3   Telephone the class

LEVEL

Elementary and above

TIME

10 minutes in the first class, 10 minutes outside class, 10 minutes in the following lesson.

AIMS

To encourage the students to make telephone calls in English to people they know.

PREPARATION

In a previous lesson, ask the students to write down their telephone numbers. Make copies of the list of telephone numbers. Warn the students that if the telephone number they are giving is not their own, they should ask permission to use it.

PROCEDURE

1 Distribute the list of telephone numbers. Tell the students they are going to telephone each other in English.

2 The class decide who each student is going to telephone: for example, the person below them in the list, or the person three lines above them, or the seventh line below.

3 The class decide on a topic they would like to discuss over the telephone—for instance, their opinions of the textbook, hobbies, and interests, or something currently in the news. They should choose a subject suitable for their current level of English.

4 Practise some of the ways of opening and closing telephone conversations in English, and some polite ways of asking for information and opinions.

5 Allow the students a few minutes at the end of the lesson to arrange when they are going to make the telephone calls to their partners. (Each student will receive one telephone call and initiate one.) Explain that after they have made the telephone call, they should write down how they felt about making the call, and what information and opinions they received on the topic they talked about—a kind of 'telephone log'. They will hand this log in to the teacher in the next class.

6 The students make their telephone calls at home and note down their reactions in their log.

7 During the next class, collect the logs and also ask for some verbal feedback on the calls.

COMMENTS

The logs ensure that the students do the activity and also that they reflect on it. If a student does not have a telephone, they could use a public telephone or you could arrange for the student and his/her telephone partner to do the activity as a conversation after class. This activity is a good one for a new class, because it helps them to get to know each other, and it can be repeated several times, using different methods of selecting the students to telephone.

6.4 Telephone voting

LEVEL

Elementary and above

TIME

10 minutes in class, 5 minutes outside class, 5 minutes in the next class.

AIMS

To understand information given over the telephone by familiar voices.

PROCEDURE

1 Show students the press cutting below, and ask them what the people mentioned in the article are going to do and why. You might need to explain what Christmas carols are if the students are not familiar with the term.

Vote for your favourite carol
and help leukaemia research

At this time of year people start to sing or hum their favourite carol. But which is the nation's most popular? We'd like TV Times readers to vote for their favourite from the list on the right. Not only will you be helping to discover the nation's favourite carol, but the seven most popular will form the programme for the TV Times Carol Concert in aid of the Leukaemia Research Fund. Lines are open from 14 Nov until midnight on 26 Nov and calls will cost approximately 10p.

PICK YOUR WINNER

O come all ye faithful	0891 137 640
Good King Wenceslas	0891 137 641
Away in a manger	0891 137 642
It came upon the midnight clear	0891 137 643
Once in royal David's city	0891 137 644
Silent night	0891 137 645
Hark the herald angels sing	0891 137 646

(from *TV Times*)

2 Tell the class that they are going to conduct their own telephone vote, but they will not know the topic until they telephone their 'vote collector' this evening. When the students telephone their 'vote collector', he or she will tell them the topic they are voting on, give them four choices, and note down their name and how they voted.

3 Ask a few students to volunteer as 'vote collectors'. They will receive about eight telephone calls at home and report back in the next class on the information they have collected. (So, if they are children or teenagers, it might be a good idea to warn parents and get their permission first!)

4 Assign each 'vote collector' about eight members of the class, and make sure that they write down his/her telephone number. Arrange to meet the vote collectors secretly at the end of the class.

5 Tell the class that when they telephone, they must speak in English. Elicit/give them a model of a possible conversation in which they greet each other politely, ask the vote collector what the topic is, give their opinion, and close the conversation politely. They practise the conversation in pairs.

6 Decide on a particular time that evening when the telephone calls will be made, for example, between 7.00 p.m. and 8.00 p.m.

7 At the end of the lesson, decide with the vote collectors what the class are going to vote on—for example, which they prefer of four songs, or film stars, or on a political decision which is currently in the news.

8 The vote collectors write down the choices and make a chart to record the votes. Make sure they include the name and the vote in each case.

9 In the next lesson, the vote collectors report back on how the vote went, and all the votes are counted to get a final result for the class.

VARIATION	This activity could also be used to see how many people know the answer to a grammar problem, or a joke, or some general knowledge questions.
COMMENTS	**1** This is a good activity for young teenagers.
	2 The activity works better if the students do not know in advance what they are going to vote on, so that they need to talk on the telephone more. It also means that they cannot prepare an answer in advance (in contrast to 6.3 above which is therefore an easier activity) and therefore have to answer there and then. If you want to make it easier for elementary students you could let them know the topic in advance.

6.5 Answering machines

LEVEL	**Intermediate and above**
TIME	**30 minutes**
AIMS	**To understand answering machines.**
MATERIALS	A tape recorder. A few messages of the kind left on answering machines. Either record them yourself (you do not need to actually have an answering machine) or use some examples from published material (for example, *Listening Elementary*, Unit 2, or *Listening Intermediate*, Unit 3, in the Oxford Supplementary Skills series). 10–15 pictures of different kinds of people from magazines and newspapers (depending on the size of the class).
PROCEDURE	**1** Ask the students whether they like answering machines. Do they have one themselves? What do they do when they telephone somebody and get an answering machine? Do they remember some particularly good or irritating answering machines? What about music, funny voices, or funny messages?
	2 Play the answering machine messages and ask the students to note down and compare any clues they hear about the recipient's
	– family
	– friends
	– work

– hobbies and interests
– age
– habits and lifestyle.
You will probably need to play the messages more than once.

3 Divide the students into groups of four or five and give each
   group a picture of a person. Ask them to decide what kind of
   person this is, using the categories in Step 2 above.

4 Each member of the group should now prepare a short
   message to leave on this person's answering machine. The
   message should illustrate some aspect of the 'life' they have
   constructed for the person in the picture.

5 Groups now take it in turn to record their messages.

6 Collect the pictures of the people and stick them up where all
   the class can see them.

7 Play the recordings the students have made. The class have to
   decide which answering machine belongs to each of the people.

FOLLOW-UP

In pairs the students design and record in English the message
they would leave on their own answering machine. Elicit some of
the things they should bear in mind, for example, that many
people try to give as little information as possible, so that burglars
cannot take advantage.

COMMENTS

This activity encourages the students to construct an image of an
unseen speaker and in this way lessens the gap between the sender
and recipient of this type of spoken message.

6.6 Real-life telephoning

LEVEL

Intermediate and above

TIME

**15 minutes in class, 10–15 minutes outside class, 15 minutes
in class.**

AIMS

**To understand information given over the telephone; to
make telephone calls to people the students do not know.**

PREPARATION

Design a number of tasks in which the students have to find out
information by telephoning. There should be at least one for every
3–4 students. If possible try to make as many as possible of the
tasks local or 'freephone numbers' to save the students spending
money on the calls. It is also a good idea to make them public
service numbers, or ones where the receivers deliberately
advertise their number because they want to sell something, so
that the students cannot be accused of being a nuisance. It is also

useful to make the telephone calls yourself first to check for any difficulties the students may have. In an English-speaking country a list of tasks could look like this:

Telephone task sheet

1 Telephone some major stores in the town to get full details about which night(s) they stay open late and for how long.

2 Find out the number of the local blood donor service, and ask when and where the next donation session will take place.

3 Find out the number of your local Member of Parliament and ring to check when and where his/her 'surgery' for constituents takes place.

4 Ring three taxi companies in the town (try to use their 'freephone' numbers) and find out how much they charge for a trip from where you are staying to the nearest airport. Is there much difference in the price?

5 Ring up the local railway station and find out the latest train you can take back from London to your town on a Sunday.

6 Ring a local tourist attraction (for example, a castle, a country park, or a heritage centre) and ask about opening times and prices of admission.

7 Ring the weather line the night before your next lesson and note down the weather forecast for the next day. Was it accurate?

8 Ring the local tourist information line and note down three interesting events which are happening in the town, with dates, times, and venues.

9 Find the numbers of two video rental companies from the Yellow Pages. Ring them up and find out how much it costs per month to rent a video machine.

10 You want to give an English friend a compact disc by your favourite singer or group. Ring the local record shops to find out if they have got it in stock.

Photocopiable © Oxford University Press

If you are working in a country where English is not used as a working language, you can still find a lot of sources, such as the UK, US, or Australian Embassies, the British Council, multinational companies, international hotels, banks, airlines, travel firms, and tourist information recorded in English, which you can use for telephone tasks. You can also ask English-speaking colleagues or friends if they would mind pretending to be the railway station or the local record shop and allowing one or two students to ring them at a specified time one night. Provide your colleagues with a card with the information written on it so that the favour is not too onerous!

PROCEDURE

1 Distribute the telephone task sheet and either assign, or allow the students to choose one of the tasks.

2 Revise the conventions of using the telephone in an English-speaking culture and on polite ways of asking for information. Less confident students may prefer to role-play the telephone calls before making them in reality.

3 The students have a specified number of days (say three) in which to telephone and find out the information.

4 Conduct feedback on the tasks. For example, ask groups of students to design a wall poster for tourists featuring the information they have collected. You could give a prize to the most informative and attractive poster.

7 Listening projects

This chapter contains suggestions for longer activities which integrate listening with the other skills and which will need more than one lesson to complete. The aim of these activities is to give the students the chance to put into practice all the skills they have learnt in previous chapters. The students are expected to work independently and co-operatively, managing their own activities, with the teacher in an advisory role. The activities forge links between the classroom and the world outside it, and in many of the activities, the students will need to leave the classroom to collect their listening material, either inside class time or in addition to it. In this way, they can use the listening skills they have learnt in the classroom 'for real'.

7.1 Interview for a magazine

LEVEL

Lower-intermediate and above

TIME

At least two 50-minute lessons

AIMS

To encourage accurate listening; to integrate listening with the other three skills; to encourage the students to work independently; to edit and change a listening text for use in another medium.

MATERIALS

Tape recorders and microphones.

PREPARATION

Identify some people in the school or town who can speak English. They do not need to be native speakers as long as the interviews are conducted in English. Ask them if they would mind being interviewed for a student magazine. The number of interviewers needed will depend on the size of the class—you will need roughly one speaker for every four to five students. A portable tape recorder for each group of students with recording facilities to record their interview.

PROCEDURE

1 Divide the students into groups of four or five. Explain that each group is going to be responsible for writing an article for a class magazine. The articles will be based on interviews. Decide on a name for the magazine.

2 Each group chooses or is assigned an interviewee. Tell the students a few details about the interviewee—where they live, job, age, and so on.

3 With the students, look at a typical interview of a star in a teenage magazine and notice what kinds of questions are asked—for example, favourite music, food, hobbies, family, attitudes to the opposite sex. The students decide which of these questions it might be appropriate (or inappropriate!) to ask their interviewee.

4 The students draw up a list of questions they are going to ask their interviewee. They should ask you to check their English before they do the interview.

5 Next, the groups arrange to meet their interviewee and record their interview.

6 The students now have to transcribe and edit their interview before it can be published in written form. They do not have enough space to use all the information in the recording so they need to choose what to keep. They also need to listen carefully to get some direct quotes. Hand them the sheet of instructions below and tell them that they must work together independently through the steps, although of course they can ask the teacher for help at any point if they get stuck. Note: you can omit Step 2 if the students have not yet learnt about reported speech.

Interview for _____ Magazine

1

a Choose one person in the group to be the writer.

b Listen to your interview and choose the TWO answers that interested you most. What were the questions which went with them?

c Write down the two questions and answers (one person writes, the others listen and dictate).

d Check with the teacher that you have got all the words and have spelt them correctly.

2

a Change writers.

b Put the two questions and answers into reported speech.
Begin 'We asked him/her if ... ', 'He or she said that ...'
One person writes and the others read and suggest changes.

c Check with the teacher that you have done it correctly.

3

a Change writers.

b Listen to the interview again and note down:
   – something interesting about the interviewee's past
   – something interesting about the interviewee's present
   – something interesting about the interviewee's future
   (You may find that the interviewee does not mention them all.)

One person should make notes, the others make suggestions about what to write down.

Unlike Steps 2 and 3, you do not need the exact words, just the ideas.

4

a Change writers again.

b You now have enough material to write the article (one person writes, the others make suggestions). It should be between 200 and 300 words long.

1 Begin with the interviewee's *name* and *job*.

2 Then mention the *place* where you interviewed them.

3 If you like, mention some details about their *appearance* or *age*.

4 Then mention the interesting things about their *past, present*, and *future*.

5 Somewhere in the article, include the two direct quotes you wrote down in Steps 1 and 2.

6 Include any other details you want.

7 Sign your names at the end of the article.

Photocopiable © Oxford University Press

COMMENTS

A good activity for young teenagers and for students whose English is not yet at a very high level.

Acknowledgements

I first saw Jerome Boulter and Maria Meusz do this with a class in Coimbra, Portugal.

FOLLOW-UP 1

Many schools produce actual magazines in English—this could be part of such a project.

FOLLOW-UP 2

If the students' first attempts at recording do not come out well, or after a 'trial run', you can give them a quiz like the one below. It would be useful in the following activities from this book:

and the rest of the activities in this chapter. For elementary students, you might want to translate the quiz into their first language. Adapt it to include any problems the students had with their recordings.

Quiz on making recordings

1 What can you do if you get these problems while you are recording?
   - lots of hissing 's' sounds when people speak
   - the sound of rustling paper when people refer to notes
   - lots of background noise from the corridor outside
   - a clicking noise when you operate the on/off button
   - the sound of the wind when recording out of doors.

True or false?

2 Indoors, the best place to make a recording is a big room where you have space to set out all your recording equipment. T/F

3 You need a separate microphone, not one that is included in the tape recorder. T/F

4 Your speakers should sit about 30 cm away from the microphone. T/F

5 If your sound meter is registering –3, you are in trouble. T/F

6 When you are interviewing outside, you should put the microphone as close as possible to the speaker's face. T/F

Photocopiable © Oxford University Press

Answers

1 Solving problems: for detailed answers to these questions, refer to Appendix 1, page 133.
2 False   3 True   4 True
5 False. This is within the acceptable range of sound (see Appendix 1).
6 False. This might seem rather aggressive and put the interviewee off, and produce a lot of unpleasant /s/, /p/, and /b/ sounds. On the other hand, you should not be too far away either.

7.2 Voice of the people

LEVEL

Lower-intermediate and above

TIME

10 to 15 minutes in class, 1 hour outside class, 20 minutes' feedback in class.

AIMS

To practise asking questions; to listen to and summarize information gathered.

MATERIALS

Portable tape recorders and microphones for the students to record their interviews.

PREPARATION

If you can, record an example of the kind of interview described in Procedure, Steps 1 and 2 from an English-language station or, failing that, a station broadcasting in their own language, to show the students what it is like.

PROCEDURE

1 Explain to the students that radio and television stations often go out on to the streets to ask members of the public their opinion on some controversial topic which is in the news at the moment, such as women priests, or the imprisonment of a famous footballer for attacking a fan.

2 Point out or elicit that the interviews are typically very short, consisting of just one main question and answer before the interviewer moves on to another person.

3 Together the class decide on a controversial topic and prepare a question to ask the people they are going to interview. The local and national news will provide plenty of ideas for 'hot' topics.

4 Rehearse a polite explanation of what they are doing which they can give to the people they interview. Stress the importance of being courteous.

5 The students carry out their interviews outside class, in groups of two or three, taking it in turns to ask the question. If they are in a non-English-speaking country, they will still be able to find English speakers, either by prefacing their questions with 'Excuse me, do you speak English?' or by you arranging for them to interview English-speaking people you know. They will probably be able to find a lot of English speakers within the school itself. About 10 to 15 opinions should be sufficient. Remind the students that the answers should be short and snappy! It is a good idea for them to test that their machine is recording at the correct sound level after doing the first interview—there is nothing more dispiriting than doing a whole series of recordings and then finding that they are inaudible.

6 After they have made the recording, the students should listen to it and prepare a short introduction and summary. This could include:

   – what they wanted to find out
   – percentages of people who held particular points of view
   – whether they were surprised by their findings
   – what reasons they can suggest for their findings.

7 The students present their interviews in class, introducing the recording before they play it. Allow time for class discussion afterwards.

VARIATION

At Step 5, instead of preparing a summary, the students could design comprehension questions for the rest of the class to answer while they listen to the recording.

7.3 Desert island discs backwards

LEVEL	**Intermediate and above**
TIME	**30 minutes in one lesson, 30 minutes to record in the next lesson**
AIMS	**To integrate listening with the other three skills.**
MATERIALS	Tape recorder (optional).

PREPARATION

1 If you have access to British radio, record a short excerpt of the programme *Desert Island Discs*. (BBC Enterprises also has a video version of the programme for sale—see Appendix 2.)

2 Collect 8–10 magazine pictures of non-famous people.

PROCEDURE

1 Ask the students to write on a piece of paper the name of some music they have at home which they either like very much or hate. Collect in the papers.

2 Show the students the magazine pictures and tell them they are going to make a radio programme about one of these people. Ask the class to choose one of the pictures.

3 Pin the picture on the board and ask the class to imagine some facts about the person's life. For example:
   – He or she is famous for something. What is it?
   – Does he or she have a family?
   – What kind of personality does he or she have?
   – What are his/her interests?
   – Did he or she have a hard or easy life?

4 Explain to the students that the programme they are going to make is like one that has been running on British radio for a number of years. In the programme, a famous person is interviewed about their life, usually starting with their childhood, and is also asked to choose eight pieces of music which mean a lot to them, and which remind them of particular times in their lives. Play an excerpt from the programme if it is available.

5 Select a piece of paper for every 3–4 students at random from the ones you have collected and read out the names of the pieces of music.

6 Assign two or three students to each piece of music. One of the students should be the one who chose that piece of music.

7 In their groups, the students decide why the person in the picture might have chosen this piece of music, and what time or event in that person's life it reminds them of. They should write a short paragraph in the role of the person, in which he or she

explains why this piece of music is particularly significant. Circulate and help with language. Collect in the paragraphs at the end of the lesson.

8   The students who wrote down the music should bring it from home to the next lesson, when the 'programme' will be recorded.

9   In the next lesson, you or the class should choose one student to be the famous person, and one student to be the interviewer. Give the famous person the paragraphs. While he or she is reading them silently, decide with the rest of the class what the most logical 'running order' for the pieces of music should be.

10 The students perform the programme, with the interviewer asking the famous person why he or she has chosen the pieces of music. Pause after each reply and play an excerpt of the music; the group who were assigned it are responsible for cueing and playing the excerpt. If you have a tape recorder, the performance can be recorded and added to your tape library (see 2.12).

FOLLOW-UP

The groups might like to follow this by making a similar programme based on one of their teachers, or an English-speaking person in their community, or on one of their fellow students.

VARIATION

The BBC World Service has another programme called *Slow Train*, using excerpts of literature instead of music, which the students might like to listen to and copy.

7.4 Making a news broadcast

LEVEL

Intermediate and above

TIME

50 minutes

AIMS

To integrate listening with the other three skills.

MATERIALS

A tape recorder; snippets from a newspaper.

PREPARATION

1   Before the students do this activity, it will help if they have had practice in some of the different kinds of reporting it contains:

Interviews:	5.6	The news expanded
	7.1	Interview for a magazine
	7.2	Voice of the people
Advertisements:	5.11	Radio advertisements
Sports:	5.9	Sports temperatures
Weather:	5.8	Weather diary
Headlines:	5.4	Shortening the news

PREPARATION

2 Prepare a card for each group of four students on which you have stuck short snippets from a newspaper including:

   – the first few lines of a news item
   – the first bit of an advertisement
   – the first bit of a weather report
   – the first bit of a sports report.

If you are in an English-speaking country or if there is a local English-language paper, snippets from the local newspaper work well, because the students may already know some of the background details.

Example

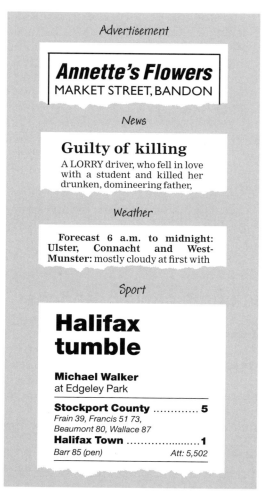

PROCEDURE

1 Ask the students to get into groups of four and give each group a card.

2 Give the students a time limit (say 30 minutes) in which they must prepare a short news report plus a commercial break with advertisements based on the items on their card. They can

use their imaginations and develop the items in any way they like. All the students must take part in the recording.

3 Circulate and give any help that is needed.

4 When the students are ready, they should record their news programmes.

5 Play some of the recordings so that the other students can hear them.

VARIATION

Once the students have had experience of making this kind of recording, they might like to have some fun with the idea, and go on to make a similar news broadcast for the year 2050, or a hundred years ago.

Acknowledgements
Brian Quigley, a CTEFLA trainee in Cork, gave me the idea for this activity.

7.5 A radio play

LEVEL

Intermediate and above

TIME

50–90 minutes (can be homework) plus 30–45 minutes in a later lesson.

AIMS

To integrate listening with the other three skills; to make the students aware of the effectiveness of radio as a medium for drama.

MATERIALS

Tape recorders and microphones; handout from the next page.

PREPARATION

If you can, record 2–3 minutes of a radio play in English, and make a transcript of what the characters say. Recordings of radio plays are also available on cassette.

PROCEDURE

1 (Optional) If you have been able to record part of a radio play in English, play it to the students first without showing them the transcript and ask them to imagine where the action is taking place, what it is about, and what the characters look like, judging by their voices and what they say.

2 (Optional) Give the students a copy of the transcript and play the excerpt again. Ask the students if the transcript gives them any more help in answering the questions. These two steps should show the students how much information a good writer for drama on radio is able to convey through dialogue alone.

3 Distribute the handout on the next page.

Young writers' competition
Write for radio!
KITCHEN TALK

Everybody knows that 'everything' happens in the kitchen.
Every home has kitchen stories—some are funny, some are
tragic, most are a rich source of human characters and
interest.

Rules of the competition

Scripts

1 All scripts must be written for radio production.

2 Scripts should be 4–5 minutes in duration.

   Make sure that you 'act' through your script, rather than just
   read it, in order to time it accurately.

Characters

3 Scripts must be written for 2 or 3 characters only.

   They can be of any age, background, or gender.

Setting

4 The action must be set in a kitchen, anywhere you like. All the
   action will take place in this confined space.

Subjects

5 You can choose any subject—from gossip to science fiction—
   but it will probably make better drama if it contains some
   conflict, misunderstanding, or difference in points of view.

Closing date

6 Send us your script and a tape of it in performance by_____
   [teacher to fill in date].

4 Divide the class into small groups of three, four, or five and tell
   them that they are going to prepare and record a short play.

5 Advise the students that the best way to prepare their play is
   not to try to start writing it down immediately. The best
   procedure is to think of what kind of incident or discussion
   could happen in a kitchen between two or three people:

   – what time of day is it?
   – where is the kitchen and what does it look like?
   – is this happening in the past, present, or future?
   – what do the people look like? speak like?
   – what are they doing in the kitchen?

   Only when they have decided on these points will it be a good
   idea to try improvising the conversation that takes place. They
   will also need one person to make notes, not of the exact words
   that are said, but of the main outline, for example: *a mother and*

father are discussing their daughter—they are very worried about her. She will not eat anything and they think she may have anorexia—she comes into the kitchen—they quickly change the subject and pretend to be talking about ...

6 The group will need to act out the dialogue twice, once to get the outline, the second to time it and discuss if necessary how they can extend it or cut it down to fit the 5-minute time limit. They will need to make sure that it contains the following stages:

- setting the scene
- establishing the problem or conflict
- the problem or conflict gets more complicated
- some sort of crisis or climax
- the problem or conflict is solved, although that might lead to a new problem.

7 When they have rehearsed their play, they should record it, adding any necessary sound effects such as opening and closing music, kitchen sounds, and credits. If they make a mistake while recording, they can always stop, rewind, and re-record.

8 **(Optional)** If they want to, at this point they can listen to their recording and transcribe it to provide a tapescript for the play.

9 In the next class, the recordings are played to the whole class. The class can vote for the best one.

VARIATION

If you do not have recording facilities, the students can perform their plays for each other, adding sound effects as in Activity 2.4.

FOLLOW-UP

The tapescripts can be passed to groups in another class, who can try acting out and recording the play and then comparing their version with the original recording.

COMMENTS

1 A double cassette tape recorder, which will allow recording from one cassette on to another, is useful but not essential for adding sound effects.

2 The recordings can be added to the tape library (see 2.12).

7.6 Local radio

LEVEL

Intermediate and above

TIME

20 minutes for preparation, 30–40 minutes for planning and recording (this can be homework), 30 minutes in class

AIMS

To integrate listening with the other three skills.

MATERIALS

Tape recorder and microphones. Copies of the advert for a local radio station: one for every 5–6 students.

RADIO ALBA
Your friendly local radio station 24 hours live!

Interviews   Live phone-ins   All kinds of music from classical to country, rock to rap

225 FM

Fun for children   What's on and where

Competitions and requests   Books to buy   News and views

TUNE IN—WE'LL MAKE YOU GRIN

Photocopiable © Oxford University Press

PREPARATION

1 It will help if the students have done some of the earlier activities on various types of radio programme before they tackle this activity.

2 If you have a local radio station, for instance, a hospital station, or one based in the local university, or a small local commercial station, find out what they do.

PROCEDURE

1 Divide the class into groups of five or six and give them copies of the advertisement. Ask them whether they have ever heard of this kind of radio station, serving a small special audience. Do they know of any local radio stations in the area? Tell the students about any information you have found out.

2 Ask the students to look again at the advertisement, and say whether they think the kinds of programmes offered fit the audience they are aimed at. What kind of programmes would they offer if they were planning a radio station to serve the local hospital? How would they compare with the advertisement?

3 Tell the groups that they are going to bid for the franchise, i.e. to become the broadcasting company for a local radio station—it could be for the local hospital, or for their school, or their area. The class as a whole should decide which kind of local radio station they want to be.

4 Each group plans and records excerpts from the programmes they would offer for a 'demo' tape. The tape should be no longer than 4–5 minutes. They can also prepare a 'flyer' like the one shown to go with their tape.

5 The students play their tapes in class and vote on who made the best tape and should get the radio franchise.

VARIATION

If you do not have recording facilities, they can perform their 'demos' for each other.

7.7 Oral history

LEVEL

Intermediate and above

TIME

30 minutes, 30 minutes outside class, 30 minutes in the next lesson.

AIMS

To help the students to compare the information that they hear.

MATERIALS

A tape recorder.

PREPARATION

You will need some English-speaking people from an older generation than the students for them to interview. See 6.6 for suggestions about where to find English speakers if you live in a non-English-speaking country. The students will also be able to help you find people to interview.

PROCEDURE

1 Ask the students to note down what comes into their head when they remember these things from their childhood:

games   school   music   food   clothes   prices   family entertainment   transport   *do*s and *don't*s about behaviour weather

2 Ask the students to get into pairs and compare what they wrote. Do they notice any similarities or differences?

3 Tell the students that they are going to interview a person who was a child during a different era. They should prepare some questions to ask that person about their childhood, focusing on the areas you asked them about in Step 1. Circulate and help them with any language difficulties.

4 The students record a five-minute interview with their chosen person.

5 In the next class, a few students play their tapes, while the other students make notes about each of the areas mentioned. In pairs, the students compare the notes they made.

6 Go over each of the areas mentioned in Step 1, and ask the students whether they think things were better in this respect for themselves as children or for one of the people they heard on the tape.

COMMENTS

1 If the people they have recorded agree, the tapes could be added to the school's tape library (see 2.12), or used with other classes.

2 See Appendix 2 for a suggested source of oral history tapes, and Ronald Blythe's *Akenfield: Portrait of an English Village* for material which could be used as a warm-up to this activity.

Appendix 1
How to make good quality recordings

Many of the activities in this book ask the students or teacher to make audio recordings. You may find the following suggestions useful for ensuring that you get good sound quality.

Indoor recording

The room

1 Choose a quiet room if possible—not too near the street or a noisy corridor or sports field.
2 Choose a smallish room. If you have to use a big room, try to reduce the size by screening off the area where you are going to do the recordings. You can make screens from video trolleys or movable blackboards, or clothes dryers draped with rugs, curtains, or coats to cut out echo.
3 Choose a room that has as many soft furnishings—curtains, carpets, upholstered furniture, wallpaper—as possible, to minimize the number of hard shiny surfaces that the sound can bounce off.
4 If the students want more privacy, they can construct a studio in one corner of the classroom by putting a smaller table or chairs on top of a bigger table and draping it with sheets, or blankets.

   If you are recording at home, you could put the microphone on the seat of an armchair, and drape a sheet or rug over the chair to achieve the same kind of effect.

The tape recorder

5 Most schools have tape recorders which are perfectly adequate for making recordings for the activities suggested in this book. Make sure your recorder has a counter and a sound meter, which should normally be registering the sound between −3 and −5 (Vu meter) or between −3 and +2 (PPM).

6 For editing, a double cassette recorder is useful, so that you can record from one cassette on to another.

7 It is also useful to have a radio cassette recorder to tape programmes off-air.

Microphones

8 It is essential to get a separate microphone which you can connect to your tape recorder, as built-in microphones are usually inadequate. Take your tape recorder with you when buying a microphone so that you can check that they are compatible.

Getting the sound right

9 If you are recording indoors, put the microphone on one table, on a stand, and the recorder on another table. This will cut down on machine noise from the recorder. Cover the tables with a cloth, if possible.

10 Do not put your interviewees too near the microphone: if you do, you will get 'popping' noise on sounds like /p/, /b/, and /t/ and unpleasant hissing on /s/ sounds. Try to move people a bit further away. If only the /s/ is a problem, try putting a piece of nylon over the microphone.

11 Ideally, your interviewees should be placed at an equal distance away from the microphone, about 20–30 cm. Have a sound test, and if one of the interviewees is much quieter or louder than the others, adjust his/her distance from the microphone.

12 Use the pause button to cut down on the clicking noise you can get from operating the on/off button; press it down first before you press the recording button on or off.

13 If the speakers are referring to papers, make sure they only have one sheet of paper and that they hold it, rather than shuffling and rustling papers on the table near the microphone or recorder.

Outdoor recording

14 Hand-held microphones held at shoulder height get the best sound quality, and it is a good idea to hold the microphone up to each person in turn as they speak. Try, however, not to make it seem aggressive, as this can intimidate interviewees.

15 You can buy a windsock to protect the microphone in windy conditions.

Appendix 2
Useful sources of
material

Radio

BBC World Service/BBC English
Bush House, PO Box 76, The Strand, London WC2B 4PH, UK.
Tel. (+44) (0)171 257 2886, Fax (+44) (0)171 430 1985. Make it
clear which service you are enquiring about when you write or
ring. Information about the BBC World Service schedules and
frequencies, or about BBC English programmes, is also available
from their publications, such as the magazine *BBC Worldwide* or
from their World Wide Web site:
http//:www.bbc.co.uk/worldservice/index.htm

Voice of America
Details of schedules and frequencies can be found on their World
Wide Web site http://www.voa.gov/

See also 'The Internet', below.

Audio tapes

Talking Tapes Direct
PO Box 190, Peterborough PE2 6UW, UK. Tel. (+44) (0)1773
230645, Fax (+44) (0)1773 238966. This company sells a lot of
audio recordings of programmes originally broadcast on radio
and television as well as many other audio tapes.

British Library National Sound Archive
29 Exhibition Road, London SW7 2AS, UK. Tel. (+44) (0)171
412 7405. Their oral history section has recordings on such things
as holocaust survivors, steel workers, wildlife, and period sounds.
Some are obtainable in teachers' packs from the British Library
Education Service (see below).

British Library Education Service
Great Russell Street, London WC1B 3DG,
UK. Tel. (+44) (0)171 412 7783 or 7797. They produce a
magazine called *Sources*, which includes sound recordings.

Royal National Institute for the Blind
Customer Services, PO Box 173, Peterborough PE2 6WS, UK.
Tel. (+44) (0)345 023153. For information about groups which
make audio tapes for the blind.

Television

BBC World Service Television
Satellite broadcasts worldwide. See BBC World Service under
Radio, above.

ITN World News* and *Central News
Videos of news programmes with accompanying activity books,
published by Oxford University Press. Could be used with
activities on the news in Chapter 5.

Worldnet television—Voice of America
Satellite broadcasts worldwide. See under Radio, above.

CNN video and World Wide Web materials
CNN produce *CNN Newsroom*, a 30-minute block of news
developed especially for schools. Their Web site has daily
classroom guides with a programme synopsis, questions for
discussion, classroom and homework activities, etc. Contact
Christine Alloin, CNN House, 19–22 Rathbone Place, London
W1P 1DF. Tel. (+44) (0)171 637 6912, Fax (+44) (0)171 637
6926. Web site: http://cnn.com/

Telephoning

British Telecommunications
81 Newgate Street, London EC1A 7AJ, UK. Tel. 0800 700 920.
They produce a useful free booklet on the parts played by
listeners and speakers in conversation, and also provide
illustrative phone calls (in the UK only). The text of the book is
reproduced on their Internet site http://www.talkworks.co.uk

The Internet

Song lyrics
Song lyrics can be obtained from a number of sources on the Net.
Simply type in the search term 'song lyrics', which can be refined
with the names of particular singers, etc. One good site I have
found is the International Lyrics server at http://www.lyrics.ch/
Many pop groups have 'fanzines' on the World Wide Web which
publish song lyrics and other details. Type in the name of the
group plus 'lyrics' on your search engine.

Radio on the Net

Radio programmes can be accessed via the Net but you will need RealAudio software to be able to listen. You can do this by accessing their Web site at http://www.realaudio.com/ Another site is Audionet at http://www.AudioNet.com/ CBS Radio is at http://www.cbsradio.com/ ABC Radio is at http://www.realaudio.com/contentp/abc.html

E-mail

An excellent discussion group for all language teaching queries, ideas, etc. is TESL-L. You can contact them by e-mailing listserv@cunyvm.cuny.edu

See also Radio and Television, above, and Penfriends, below.

Penfriends

I recommend that you set up links from class to class and monitor them in conjunction with the other teacher, rather than allowing individual students to correspond. This is both to ensure educational benefits, and to protect your students from unwelcome advances.

One way of finding penfriends for your students is by joining the TESL-L discussion group (see above). Another way is to find out if your town has twinning links with towns in other countries.

There are also commercial organizations which you can register with to find penfriends. Some examples are:

I*EARN

Contact person: Lisa Jobson, I*EARN, 475 Riverside Drive, Suite 540, NY 10115, USA. Tel. (+1)212/870 2693, Fax (+1)212/870 2672, e-mail: <iearn@iearn.org>, World Wide Web site http://www.iearn.org/iearn

The Penpal Box at Kids' Space

This World Wide Web site allows both individuals and classes to advertise for pen friends. Their Web site is http://www.KS-connection.com

The International Pen Friends Service

Lorrin L. Lee, 2357 Beretania Ste 750, Honolulu, HI 96826, USA. Tel. (+1) 808 949 5000, Fax (+1) 808 947 8817, e-mail <lorrin@global-homebiz.com>, Web site http://www.global-homebiz.com/ipf.html

See also the Appendix to *Letters*, in this series.

Bibliography

1 Books or articles mentioned in the text

★ indicates suggestions for further reading.

Allan, D. 1991. 'Tape journals: bridging the gap between communication and correction'. *ELT Journal* 45/1: 61–66.

Bailey, A. 1997. *Talkworks.* British Telecommunications plc. Pages 53–76 give good, practical advice on how to be a good listener in conversations. See Appendix 2 for address.

Baker, A. 1981. *Ship or Sheep?* Cambridge: Cambridge University Press.

Bell, A. 1991. *The Language of News Media.* Oxford: Blackwell.

Bell, J. 1989. *Soundings.* London: Longman.

Blythe, R. 1972. *Akenfield: Portrait of an English village.* London: Penguin.

Bone, D. 1988. *A Practical Guide to Effective Listening.* London: Kogan Page.

Haines, S. and **B. Stewart.** 1996. *New First Certificate Masterclass* (2nd edn.). Oxford: Oxford University Press.

★ **Hargie, O., C. Saunders,** and **D. Diskson.** 1981. *Social Skills in Interpersonal Communication.* Croom Helm. Chapter 8, on how to overcome obstacles to good listening, is particularly worth reading.

Kaltenboeck, G. 1994. '"Chunks" and pronunciation teaching'. *Speak Out!* (newsletter of the IATEFL Pronunciation Special Interest Group) 13.

Lynch, T. 1983. *Study Listening.* Cambridge: Cambridge University Press.

★ **Lynch, T.** 1996. 'The listening–speaking connection'. *English Teaching Professional* 1.

Maley, A. and **A. Duff.** 1979. *Sounds Intriguing.* Cambridge: Cambridge University Press.

Maley, A., A. Duff. and **F. Grellet.** 1988. *The Mind's Eye.* Cambridge: Cambridge University Press.

Nolasco, R. 1987. *Listening Elementary.* Oxford Supplementary Skills Series. Oxford: Oxford University Press.

Randles, J. 1995. *Strange but True?* Casebook. London: Pratkus.

★ **Rost, M.** 1990. *Listening in Language Learning.* London: Longman.

★ **Rost, M.** 1994. *Introducing Listening.* London: Penguin. Read the second Rost book first, going on to the more detailed 1990 book next. Both are essential works on listening.

Scarborough, D. 1984. *Reasons for Listening*. Cambridge: Cambridge University Press.

Soars, J. and **L. Soars.** 1986. *Headway Intermediate*. Oxford: Oxford University Press.

Swan, M. and **C. Walter.** 1990. *The New Cambridge English Course 1*. Cambridge: Cambridge University Press.

Swan, M. and **C. Walter.** 1992. *The New Cambridge English Course 3*. Cambridge: Cambridge University Press.

2 Other recommended reading

Anderson, A. and **T. Lynch.** 1988. *Listening*. Oxford: Oxford University Press.
One of the essential works on listening.

Dalton, C. and **B. Seidlhofer.** 1994. *Pronunciation*. Oxford: Oxford University Press.
Chapter 5, on intonation, is particularly useful.

Davis, P. and **M. Rinvolucri.** 1988. *Dictation*. Cambridge: Cambridge University Press.

Dunn, V. and **D. Gruber.** 1987. *Listening Intermediate*. Oxford Supplementary Skills series. Oxford: Oxford University Press.

Field, J. 1996a. 'Poisoned curls: Kamal to play' in Entry Points: *Papers from a Symposium of the Research, Testing and Young Learners Special Interest Groups*. Whitstable: IATEFL.
Some insights into learners' use of top-down strategies to reach understanding.

Field, J. 1996b. 'Discovering how learners listen: some uses of learner-focused video' in *Insights 1*. Whitstable: IATEFL.

Lynch, T. 1996. *Communication in the Language Classroom*. Oxford: Oxford University Press.
Chapter 5, on listening, explains, among other things, how to increase learners' interaction and negotiation with recorded material.

Ur, P. 1996. *A Course in Language Teaching*. Cambridge: Cambridge University Press.
Pages 107–18 give hints about how to introduce real-life listening into the classroom, and pages 115–18 in particular give ideas for adapting published listening material so that it meets the needs of particular groups of students.

Willis, J. 1996. *A Framework for Task Based Learning*. London: Longman.
Chapter 6 explains how students can learn from listening to themselves or others performing tasks.

Index

Other titles in the Resource Books for Teachers series

Beginners, by Peter Grundy—over 100 original, communicative activities for teaching both absolute and 'false' beginners, including those who do not know the Latin alphabet. All ages. (ISBN 0 19 437200 6)

CALL, by David Hardisty and Scott Windeatt—a bank of practical activities, based on communicative methodology, which make use of a variety of computer programs. Teenagers and adults. (ISBN 0 19 437105 0)

Class Readers, by Jean Greenwood—practical advice and activities to develop extensive and intensive reading skills, listening activities, oral tasks, and perceptive skills. All ages. (ISBN 0 19 437103 4)

Classroom Dynamics, by Jill Hadfield—a practical book to help teachers maintain a good working relationship with their classes, and so promote effective learning. Teenagers and adults. (ISBN 0 19 437096 8)

Conversation, by Rob Nolasco and Lois Arthur—more than 80 activities which develop students' ability to speak confidently and fluently. Teenagers and adults. (ISBN 0 19 437096 8)

Creating Stories with Children, by Andrew Wright—encourages creativity, confidence, and fluency and accuracy in spoken and written English. Age 7–14. (ISBN 0 19 437204 9)

Cultural Awareness, by Barry Tomalin and Susan Stempleski— activities to challenge stereotypes, using cultural issues as a rich resource for language practice. Teenagers and adults. (ISBN 0 19 437194 8)

Drama, by Charlyn Wessels—practical advice on using drama to teach spoken communication skills and literature, and to make language learning more creative and enjoyable. Teenagers and adults. (ISBN 0 19 437097 6)

Exam Classes, by Peter May—preparation for a wide variety of public examinations, including most of the main American and British exams such as TOEFL and the new UCLES exams. Teenagers and adults. (ISBN 0 19 437208 1)

Grammar Dictation, by Ruth Wajnryb—also known as 'dictogloss', this technique improves students' understanding and use of grammar by reconstructing texts. Teenagers and adults. (ISBN 0 19 437097 6)

Learner-based Teaching, by Colin Campbell and Hanna Kryszewska—over 70 language practice activities which unlock the wealth of knowledge that learners bring to the classroom. All ages. (ISBN 0 19 437163 8)

Letters, by Nicky Burbidge, Peta Gray, Sheila Levy, and Mario Rinvolucri—demonstrates the rich possibilities of letters for language and cultural study. Contains numerous photocopiables and a section on email. Teenagers and adults. (ISBN 0 19 442149 X)

Literature, by Alan Maley and Alan Duff—an innovatory book on using literature for language practice. Teenagers and adults. (ISBN 0 19 437094 1)

Music and Song, by Tim Murphey—shows teachers how 'tuning in' to their students' musical tastes can increase motivation and tap a rich vein of resources. All ages. (ISBN 0 19 437055 0)

Newspapers, by Peter Grundy—creative and original ideas for making effective use of newspapers in lessons. Teenagers and adults. (ISBN 0 19 437192 6)

Project Work, by Diana L. Fried-Booth—practical resources to bridge the gap between the classroom and the outside world. Teenagers and adults. (ISBN 0 19 437092 5)

Pronunciation, by Clement Laroy—imaginative activities to build confidence and improve all aspects of pronunciation. All ages. (ISBN 0 19 437089 9)

Role Play, by Gillian Porter Ladousse—from highly controlled conversations to improvised drama, and from simple dialogues to complex scenarios. Teenagers and adults. (ISBN 0 19 437095 X)

Self-Access, by Susan Sheerin—helps teachers with the practicalities of setting up and managing self-access study facilities. Teenagers and adults. (ISBN 0 19 437099 2)

Storytelling with Children, by Andrew Wright—thirty stories plus hundreds of exciting ideas for using any story to teach English to children aged 7 to 14. (ISBN 0 19 437202 2)

Translation, by Alan Duff—provides a wide variety of translation activities from many different subject areas. Teenagers and adults. (ISBN 0 19 437104 2)

Very Young Learners, by Vanessa Reilly and Sheila M. Ward—advice and ideas for teaching children aged 3 to 6 years, including games, songs, drama, stories, and art and crafts. (ISBN 0 19 437209 X)